MS. CALCULATED

A DATING PLAN SO EASY
A TEENAGER CAN DO IT

TRACIE HITZ

DEDICATION

Writing this book has been my life-long dream, so this book is dedicated in memory of my brother, Michael Hitz, whose own dreams were cut short when he lost his battle with cancer in 2014. He was my buddy, my cheerleader, and my inspiration. He was my Plus One whenever I needed someone amazing to tag along to an event. He was the one who showed me that it's okay to single.
That it's amazing to be single!

He taught me so many life lessons, especially during our last ten years together. His Top 5 pieces of brotherly advice that applied to dating and to all of life inspired this book.
1) There's no such thing as perfection
2) Learn from the past, don't dwell on it
3) You don't have to be independent all the time
4) Stay positive
5) You're ready

I know you're ready too, so I'm excited to share our life lessons in this book. Thank you for supporting our dreams with this purchase. A portion of the proceeds from every book will be donated to the Michael Hitz Dream Scholarship Fund that was established to help others achieve their dreams.

CONTENTS

ACKNOWLEDGMENTS

I'm fortunate to have many people in my life that helped me achieve this dream of writing a book. This book. A special thanks goes out to Mary Hitz, Mike Hitz, Michael Hitz, Greg Bauman, Lily Hay, Aaron Villalobos, John Bacsik, Katie Louis, Brian Quinn, and Seth Godin for making a dream come true.

INTRODUCTION

"It's going to be great! We're just going to paint you purple from head to toe for our nationally televised football game against Penn State."

This was part of my pitch to sell a crazy idea to a former NFL player and a Heisman Trophy finalist to garner national attention in an effort to generate revenue at my first full-time job. After presenting everything to him, he actually agreed. And it turned out to be the most amazing moment. It defined me.

I'm the person who walks into the room with the idea that makes you think I must be joking. An idea that is completely out there, but one that is also rooted in research and strategy. I spend my time showing people how it will all come together to make sure it has a great chance at being awesome. Sure, some of my ideas have failed. Like the time I convinced Northwestern alum, Clinton Kelly from the show What Not To Wear, to do a Homecoming edition of the show to be run during a break at the football game. That definitely could've gone better, but the lessons I took away from that experience are what made me even more confident in my next idea.

I've spent my career trying to convincing people to step outside their comfort zones to do something new, something interesting. Sometimes these ideas resulted in breaking attendance records, hitting revenue goals, and/or winning national awards. One time, with the support of some amazing people, my idea to create a national Dribble to Work Day for the NCAA Women's Basketball Tournament received so much attention it landed on ESPN's SportsCenter's Top 10 Plays. Another dream come true!

I've been described by many as a connector. The person who actively seeks out the stories that can bring everyone together for unforgettable moments. I look for all of the interesting characters so we can write something that will resonate with consumers. As I was writing these stories throughout my career, I realized that my dating antics were mirroring that same marketing process. The same advice I was using to sell tickets and land clients was also working to land first dates.

Most of the marketing advice I continue to live by is from my idol, Seth Godin. He has been a huge influence in every part of my life. Reading his words and learning from his experiences gave me the information and the confidence I needed to pitch these "remarkable" ideas to people who usually needed a lot of convincing to get on board. I never gave up because he showed me what was possible. I started my Hitz & Mrs blog with the ChicagoNow community through the Tribune Publishing Company (ChicagoNow.com/hitz-mrs) based solely on the idea that Dating is Marketing. Many blog posts take Godin's advice and directly apply them to a dating scenario. My blog post titled *Seth Godin Will Marry Me* talked about why his advice is absolutely the reason I will be married one day. That blog post was one of my most read, and it even got the attention of Godin himself. My idol sent me an email after he read it. Another dream come true!

This book highlights several key moments in my life where marketing has played a pivotal role in my dating success. Without even knowing it at the time, I created and implemented a marketing plan in high school to get my first boyfriend. If you think back to a time when you were intentional about dating, I'm sure you used marketing techniques too. Throughout this book, I will share marketing advice that will help you get serious about setting a goal, creating a plan, and landing a date. Or a job. Or a dream. The advice can be catered to go after whatever you want in life.

It's always easier to accomplish a goal when you surround yourself with supportive people to hold you accountable. I want to be that person. Just for purchasing this book, you will receive access to my private Facebook Community at no extra cost. This group is the first step in creating your dating marketing plan. You will have direct access to me while I walk you through the process to get started. Plus, you will join people around the country who will share their stories that will bring us together to be supportive, strategic, positive, kind, and fun! Send an email to Tracie@HitzAndBranding.com to request access to this private Facebook Community so we can chat through the lessons in this book, and more I have to share, to see which ones will work for you. I hope to show you that Dating is Marketing so we can start writing your story together.

3

TRACIE HITZ

CHAPTER ONE

DATING IS AWKWARD

I walked into the dimly lit gym at the high school across the river. My BFF was by my side as we bobbed our heads to the song "Motown Philly" in an effort to fit into a high school that wasn't our own. We stood against the wall just inside the door as we surveyed the room to find my high school crush standing with the other jocks. He saw me. I panicked. I smiled, I think, and then I quickly looked down at the floor.

The music over the gym speakers began to fade from that upbeat Boys II Men track to Journey's slow jam, "Open Arms". This was it. This was the moment I had rehearsed a hundred times in my mind. Maybe thousands. I would walk over to him, ask him

5

to dance, and then spend those next three and a half minutes safely in his arms. But I was barely able to make my face smile a moment earlier, so getting my legs to move across the room felt nearly impossible. When I finally started moving towards him, I was going so slowly that I wasn't even sure I would actually make it to him before the song was over. Then, from what seemed like out of nowhere, I heard a voice.

"Dance?"

Somehow my high school crush was right in front of me holding his hand to guide me onto the dance floor where Journey was still playing across the speakers. He was five inches taller than me; I know this because I memorized the basketball game program at the first game of the season, so it was easy to bury my face nervously into his chest. We barely said a word as we swayed back and forth, but it was the most amazing moment. When the song ended, we let go, each took a step backwards, and waited for what seemed like an eternity for the next song to start. I secretly hoped for another slow song, but I was also extremely anxious about the thought of spending a few more minutes in his arms.

When REO Speedwagon's "Can't Fight This Feeling" started playing, we looked at each other, smiled, and each took one step forward. This time I got the courage up to ask a few questions about his basketball game that night in hopes of breaking the ice, and before I knew it, the song was over. I took one last breath of his cologne, Preferred Stock. I will never forget that smell or the memories that come flooding back whenever I smell it. It will always smell like the early 90s to me. I held my breath in hopes of one more song, but a fast song came on, people came dancing in between us, and our moment was over.

That moment was when my high school crush became my high school mission. My vision. My goal. I mean, not like in a Glenn Close *Fatal Attraction* way, but this was when I knew we had a connection that was like nothing I had ever felt before. Even though I was only 16 years old, I was sure this just had to be love. Or at least I was pretty sure it was based on all of the romantic comedies I watched over and over on my VCR. Now I just needed to figure out if he felt the same way. That's when I decided to create a plan that would allow me to spend more time with him. I thought that if he just got to know me, he would ask me to be his girlfriend. I needed a plan that made the twenty miles that stood between our two high schools seem irrelevant. This meant using my brand new driver's license as often as possible to get in front of him. I needed to find reasons to see him during the week, and especially on the weekends.

At the time, I didn't realize all of my boy-crazy plotting was actually the start of a marketing plan. I spent time looking for opportunities to see him, prepared the topics for our potential conversation, and enlisted the help of friends at my high school and his school. I had been very intentional about dating this guy. It didn't hit me until we got together for dinner almost a decade later when I was working as a marketing professional in Chicago. As we reminisced about those fun, but awkward times, I saw that the pieces I put into place back in high school were completely rooted in marketing. That everything I was learning and doing in my first full-time job was similar to what I was doing in my personal life. That I had actually been doing this my entire life. That Dating IS Marketing.

CHAPTER TWO

DATING IS SELF REFLECTION

While I now have over 20 years of marketing experience, this book will show that you don't need a marketing degree to understand and ultimately use these techniques to get a date. As I dive deeper into my Dating is Marketing process, I will start first by analyzing what was going on in that 16-year-old head of mine as it relates to the marketing principles I use everyday in my career. I always start by doing a SWOT analysis. Every project, personally or professionally, should start this way, which simply means identifying your Strengths, Weaknesses, Opportunities, and Threats. By doing this, you will figure out what is at your core, the same way you would find out what's at the core of your business.

Completing a SWOT analysis allows you to determine your vision, mission, and priorities that will guide you throughout the dating process. This exercise will help you find your way in all aspects of your life if you answer honestly, as well as ignore what everyone else thinks. It's not about who they think you should be. It's about who you want to be. Who you believe you are. Tune everybody else out when you do this exercise.

In high school, there was definitely pressure to act like everyone else even though I knew that I was different. The strategy at the time was to blend in, which actually made it possible to be myself for the most part. It wasn't always easy, but constantly checking in with myself through the years is what got me here today. This process is what gives me the confidence to believe in my crazy, strategic ideas.

SWOT ANALYSIS
16-Year-Old Tracie
July 1991

Strengths	Weaknesses
Write down what you love about yourself and your relationships.	Identify if there are any weaknesses that might be holding you back.
Positive - Honest Funny - Thoughtful Nice - Ambitious	Shy - Goody Goody Dorky - Plain Not an Athlete
Opportunities	Threats
Assess your strengths to figure out your opportunities.	Identify weaknesses to be self aware while creating a plan.
Being funny and ambitious were at the core of our connection. Going to a different school made me slightly more interesting.	Knowing the girls at his high school were pretty and outgoing pushed me outside my comfort zone.

Visit HitzAndBranding.com/minute to see my current SWOT Analysis.

Those **STRENGTHS** are still true to this day, but in high school I took some of those to the extreme. I can't remember a time I did something wrong because the thought of disappointing my parents or hurting people's feelings made me anxious. I did what I was told consistently, including being one of the few students who went to school on Senior Skip Day. NERD! That's what they called me. They meant it in a negative way, but I embraced it because that's who I was. Plus, it was better than a lot of the other labels that were put on girls in high school.

I absolutely was a nerd. I didn't just go to school on Senior Skip Day, I went to high school everyday. In fact, I never missed a day of school in my entire life. The streak started on the first day of kindergarten, so it seemed silly to break it just a few days before graduation. Plus, I felt anxious at the thought of lying to my parents and running around the city that day. I was proud of my perfect attendance, but I remember vividly the feeling of embarrassment when I was walking across my high school gym floor to receive the certificate in front of the entire school. For that moment, I let what other people think affect me. I let it dinge the self-confidence I was so desperately trying to build. Regardless of your age, it can take serious effort to keep what other people think from messing with your self confidence, so make sure you are compiling the strengths that reflect who you are, not what other people think you should be. I found that being ambitious with things like perfect attendance didn't land me into those cool cliques in school, but it's who I am at the core. It's definitely the quality that I am most proud of to this day. It defines me.

Being that goody goody growing up came across as a **WEAKNESS** because I didn't know how to position it as a strength. I loved being thoughtful and nice, but it came across as being boring and a pushover. I was extremely shy, so that made me seem unapproachable because my classmates assumed that I believed I was too good to do what everyone else was doing. I was different from most. I never went to any of the parties, even the handful I was actually invited to, because I didn't want to get in trouble. I didn't earn any cool points by separating myself from the kids who ran the school. They were nice to me when they saw me, mostly because I shared a locker with the Homecoming queen, who was beautiful inside and out, but they didn't seek me out. I was an average-looking teenager despite the many bottles of Aquanet hairspray I used in an attempt to look like the women I saw on TV. Sometimes my hair was so big that I'm pretty confident I could've been in a Whitesnake video. What I thought was fitting in was actually pulling me farther way from a majority of my classmates.

So with all of that in mind, the biggest **OPPORTUNITY** I saw was to start hanging out at another high school. So dramatic! A place where I could start over as I tried to break out of my shell. Somewhere I could figure out who I wanted to be. I was able to do this because my best friend actually from another town, so all of her friends from junior high went to another high school. It was perfect. We started splitting time between the two schools, which gave me that second chance I wanted. At this other high school, the kids only saw me from time-to-time, so this created a little mystery around me. They didn't know that my freshman and sophomore years I was so obsessed with the New Kids on the Block that I plastered my school locker with their posters. They didn't know my hair used to be a frizzy mess before I discovered mousse or that I had no idea how to dress because I spent my entire life in a Catholic school uniform. I was able to take what I learned during my first two years of high school to start rebranding myself as I headed into my junior year.

When I turned down invitations to the parties at the other high school, they assumed I didn't come because I was busy going to the parties at my own school. My shyness was now being seen as interesting. Because I had this unique opportunity to start over, I knew I had no choice but to find the courage to walk across that high school gym floor to dance with my crush that night. I didn't want my weaknesses to hold me back from growing into the person I wanted to be, which already happened at my own high school. I was ordinary there, but now I had the chance to share the real me. I just needed to be brave enough to tell my story.

Along with this opportunity came some **THREATS**, especially the other girls in school. Even with my makeover, I still wasn't acting like most of the popular girls. They were my biggest threat because they looked and acted the part of a cool high school girl. They were pretty, outgoing, and fun. Everybody wanted to be around them. The girls at the other high school also had the advantage because I didn't spend much time there. They were cheerleaders, dancers, and athletes so they spent a lot of time with my high school crush. From what I could tell when I was in their world, there were several girls trying to get his attention because he was a standout athlete. They didn't worried about other people, and I never saw them shy away from a conversation. My competition was right in front of me, so I just needed to figure out how to compete. It was extremely motivating to see their confidence, and that's in part what helped me go outside of my comfort zone in an effort to get his attention. I didn't want to miss my opportunity because I let one of my threats take what I wanted. The key is understanding your SWOT so you can stay true to yourself while finding the best ways to share your story. This is marketing.

Taking time to see the big picture is what sets you up for success. With the fear of rejection (and failure) always looming, especially for a teenager, having a solid plan is what calms my inner voice, the one that usually casts doubt about my new adventures. Of course, I was also intimidated by the beautiful cheerleaders, and my stomach would tie up in knots whenever I saw them talking to my high school crush. Sometimes seeing them with him would get me fired up enough to have the courage to talk to him while other times I felt defeated watching them all laughing together. While it was motivating to be aware of my competition, it was imperative that I didn't let comparisons hold me back. I couldn't change who I was based on what they were doing.

Another obstacle that can get in the way if we let it is allowing past experiences to affect whether or not we decide to take the risk to go after what we want. Thinking about how things went wrong in a past relationship can make a similar action seem terrifying. Luckily, at this point in my life, I didn't have any past experiences. I wasn't allowed to date until I was 16 years old so being the rule follower that I was, I never even tried. Sure, I had some crushes in junior high that never amounted to anything, but they were so childish that it didn't affect what I was feeling in high school. Because of that, I brought a positive attitude into the situation along with my naïve belief that once my high school crush had the chance to spend some time with me, he would see that we were meant to be together.

Oh, to be young again! We can't go back in time, but we can make a conscious effort to not let the past dictate our future. We need to live in the now to create a plan that sets us on the path towards everything we want in life. Looking at my 16-year-old perceived weaknesses (shy, goody-goody, dorky, plain, not an athlete), my best shot at success was to align myself with someone who appreciated these things about me. Even though I didn't know a lot about my crush, everything I did know led me to believe that he could be that someone who could love all the quirks that go along with me. I knew there wasn't anything I could do to get the coolest guys in school to notice me, and that was absolutely okay! In fact, it was better than okay because even if I were able to get a date with one of them, it would fizzle out pretty quickly because I wasn't the life of the party, the kid who would play pranks on classmates, or any of those other things that put teenagers into that cool category in high school.

So while my high school crush was an athlete, I had done enough research to know that he wasn't like the others. Keep in mind that this research was all done before social media existed so I pieced it together very slowly, and not so subtly, through mutual friends and by attending a lot of events at his school. Not having social media, I was forced to involve other people to get information rather than having the ability to follow him more anonymously online to get it. This was definitely how he became aware of my interest in him. I may have been shy, but I definitely wasn't stealth. So as embarrassing as it was at the time that people were talking nonchalantly about my feelings for him, it was actually the main reason he asked me to "Dance?" in the high school gym that night.

Of course, some kids didn't even realize the information they were feeding to me helped formulate my marketing plan. His classmates who saw things as his weaknesses were actually strengths in my mind. When they said things with a negative tone, like he doesn't drink, he never goes to parties, and he's always making dorky jokes, I just had to smile. Every new thing I learned about him strengthened my belief that it would be worth the risk of pursuing him because he was someone I knew I would love being around. He was beyond cool in my eyes. Taking the time on the front end to figure out who I was made it easy to see the type of person who would be right for me. Knowing what I wanted made it possible to devise a plan for going after it. This is one of many examples in my life that shows if you don't know where you want to go, then you won't know how to get there. Sounds pretty obvious, but often times people think they know where they are going, but they are completely off track. They are going where people tell them to go rather than where they truly want to be.

I've updated my SWOT many times since high school as I've grown into the person I am today. The core values are still intact as it's not often that we change drastically unless we've experienced a traumatic event. Sometimes we let other people make us think we are a different person, so be sure to keep tracking on your core values through the SWOT analysis process. It's also beneficial to keep tabs on the opportunities and threats because those will continue to change as you grow. Being able to track on that through the years is how I navigated all aspects of my life, but definitely my love life. It's how I've stayed positive during a long dating life.

CHAPTER THREE

DATING IS KNOWING
WHAT YOU WANT

I started learning how to go after what I wanted at a very young age. My family taught me that. One of the earliest memories I have of putting a plan into action is going to church with my dad and one of my brothers on Sunday mornings. If we behaved, which meant not tormenting each other so much that we caused a scene, we could pick out any candy we wanted at the General Store after Mass. So no surprise here, this goody goody got those Reese's Pieces every single time. My dad set out the parameters for earning the candy, so it was up to me to make it happen. My mom had no idea. It wasn't until my parents' 50th wedding anniversary celebration that my mom found out that he had been bribing us. She saw bribery, I saw a life lesson.

At the 50th Anniversary dinner party, I told the history of my parents' relationship using candy. I was able to highlight some of their most memorable moments, starting when they met at six years old, through the evolution of candy. There were life lessons learned, moments to be shared, and milestones to be celebrated around candy in our family. As I was sharing these examples, my mom looked at me very seriously.

"So that's why you always wanted to go to church with your dad?"

Well, not always. No doubt I loved Reese's Pieces, but I loved spending time with my dad even more. My dad provided a way to get something I wanted, so it was a win-win to go to church with him on Sundays. My mom also did her fair share of teaching me about goal setting with all of the activities she encouraged me to get involved in as a kid, from dance lessons to piano lessons to sports to the 4-H Club. Even my grandpa had a hand in teaching me about setting a goal, creating a plan, and most of all, putting in the work to make it happen. It was that mindset that helped me win three state titles in woodworking before I was 13 years old. He didn't let me put in half of the effort. That wasn't a thing. I sanded and sanded and sanded until it passed his smoothness test. For him, it wasn't just about winning, but about building something that I would be proud for years to come. It was about investing in yourself and setting that bar high for life. Although we were both really excited when I won!

My dad obviously learned his work ethic from my grandpa, so having them both there to teach me was exhausting at the time, but something I will be forever grateful for having. They taught me that if I wanted something, it was up to me to take action to go get it. I couldn't throw up my hands and pout my way into the life I wanted even though I tried several times. Like when I was turning 16 and embarrassed to drive the old 1978 Mustang that both of my brothers had driven before me. The car was only three years younger than I was, it was peach, and it made a ton of noise. Sure, a Mustang sounds cool, but if you haven't seen the Mustangs of the 1970s, trust me that they weren't cool. That loud V-8 engine is one of the reasons they all loved the car, but it's exactly why I didn't like it. I was trying to blend in at high school. As a shy teenager, I just wanted to fit in and this car was definitely not helping. I told my dad that the only way I would drive this car was if it was red. I pouted as I waited for his response.

"Then paint it red."

When I saw there was no changing his mind on this one, that's exactly what we did. Sanded, painted, and sanded some more. I didn't stop until it passed my grandpa's smoothness test. I knew what I wanted, so it was up to me to make it happen. With their help of course.

As a kid, I wanted everything, but my mom was the one who tried to keep me focused on things that I truly loved instead of doing something because everyone else was doing it. She taught me to consider all of the options before making a decision so that I would thrive with something I cared about rather than giving up on something that was just a whim. When I committed to something as a kid, she never let me quit. Thankfully she found a way to show me the importance of following through because that advice is what still guides me today. Even that time I begged her to let me take ballet lessons even though she knew I wouldn't like it. At three years old she knew me so well, like she had done her own SWOT analysis on me. She knew I was being drawn in to ballet by the cool slippers, beautiful leotards, and the fun tutus. She also knew that even though I was obsessed with all types of dance, and acrobat lessons, I was going to absolutely hate taking ballet because of the slow music and tedious routines. But even when she presented these facts, my begging didn't stop. Instead of just telling me "no" or giving in because I'm sure that would've been easier than listening to me whine for days, she convinced the teacher to let me join the class as sort of a free trial. Apparently I get my sales skills from my mom! But ultimately, she was right. I hated the class. It was awful. With my unrelenting stubbornness at such a young age, I tried to stick it out, but after just a few classes I was done.

Even though I was just a child, she knew who I was at the core and guided me in a way that set me up for success. She has an amazing skill of giving support while also allowing me to make my own choices. She trusts that I will do my research on whatever the new adventure is before actually jumping into it. She taught me to think before I act, and that is exactly why I love checking in with myself with the SWOT analysis. It's quite fascinating to watch my mom's ability to build confidence with the right amount of caution that keeps you focused on the bigger picture. This goal whisperer is the reason I've had the courage to take risks in life and love. When you are confident in who you are because you surround yourself with people who push you to be better, then it's easier to take that leap on a new opportunity. These become exciting rather than scary because you know you are going down the right path. The path that was meant for you and what you are gong after. It makes walking across that high school gym worth the risk every single time.

CHAPTER FOUR

DATING IS SETTING GOALS

Once you self reflect to figure out what you want, you're ready to turn it into a SMART goal: Specific, Measurable, Attainable, Relevant, Time Bound. When I was 16 years old, I remember writing in my diary, "Go to Vice Versa Dance with Brian". This is the dance where the girl asks the guy, so I had more control over making this happen because the ask was all on me. While I liked the idea of controlling my own destiny, the thought of actually asking him out was quite scary. I found courage in writing it down. And saying it out loud. I wrote the words down in my diary so I would be sure to see it everyday.

Again, I'm just a teenager here so I didn't realize the power of writing down this goal. It gave me a sense of commitment for achieving it. What started as a wish that I daydreamed about suddenly felt real. Like I needed to take action because I saw this on my list every day in my diary. It was those consistent thoughts that kept me focused on my goal. Seeing it in writing motivated me. If I were to write that goal today as a true SMART goal, it would look similar, but just adding a few key words can make all the difference.

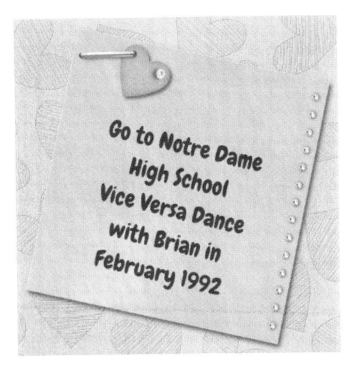

Go to Notre Dame High School Vice Versa Dance with Brian in February 1992

SPECIFIC
I picked the Vice Versa Dance because I wanted to have enough time to get to know him. This was my first real crush, so I had no idea what I was actually feeling. I just knew that I was drawn to someone as dorky as me, so I wanted to get past the awkwardness to see what this was and what it could be.

MEASUREABLE

This is pretty cut and dry. If he said "no" when I asked him to the dance, I failed. Having something measurable allows you to decide if you should give up or adjust the goal to try again.

ATTAINABLE

From the information that I gathered about him, I truly believed I had a shot at going to the Vice Versa Dance. Knowing how shy he was made it seem more likely that to get a date, I would need to be the one making the moves. Because this crush was strong, I was ready to push outside my comfort zone for a chance to spend time with him. I thought bringing him to my school for the Vice Versa Dance would take some of the pressure off since he wouldn't know anyone there. People can influence a situation without even knowing it, so spending time on my turf turned out to be a bigger advantage than I realized. Not having dozens of cheerleaders, dancers, and athletes on our first date meant I didn't have to compete for his attention. I could move at my own pace.

RELEVANT

Even before those two epic slow dances in his high school gym, I knew that going to the Vice Versa Dance would be a huge step in getting to know him. Setting the goal of going to the Vice Versa Dance is what made sense within the bigger picture, which was to hopefully become his girlfriend. That first date was the opportunity to see what could be possible. Without knowing if what I felt was real, setting a lofty goal of becoming his girlfriend didn't seem relevant. The first date was what made sense.

TIME BOUND

Having a deadline is one of the most motivating ways to get something done. There was no procrastinating on this goal because the opportunity came with an expiration date. I had to work backwards from that date of the Vice Versa Dance to make sure I had enough time to feel comfortable asking him to go with me. He also needed time to get to know me well enough to know whether or not he wanted to take this chance on me.

This crush began the summer before my junior year and the dance was in February, so I had about six months to make this all happen. That seems like an eternity when you're a kid, but when you're implementing a marketing plan involving two of the shyest people on the planet, it seemed like a pretty quick turnaround. Or maybe that was just an excuse because I was scared to actually ask him. Excuses can definitely hold us back. We can always find a reason not to do something. Taking action is hard. Doing nothing is easy. Being safe wasn't going to get me that date.

That deadline was truly motivating. Time would run out if I didn't do something. This was a time before email, cell phones, texting, and social media. I didn't go to his school, and this was back when you had to call the main house phone line that his mom was likely to answer. All of these things added a layer of anxiety that went along with this plan because the marketing options available all seemed very bold, especially to a shy teenager.

After you've created a SMART goal, the next step is committing to it. You need to truly put forth the effort to make something happen, no matter how scary it might be. People are nervous to fail while some are nervous to succeed, so you need to be honest with yourself as to whether or not you are really going to go for it. If you're not all in, you have already set yourself up for failure.

If you are committed, write it down. Put the goal in a place where you will see it everyday so you don't lose the motivation for achieving it. With my goal written in my high school diary, I saw it every single day even though I didn't have nearly enough things happening in my life to be writing with that type of frequency. But every time I wrote a journal entry, it forced me to see that goal. I didn't realize at the time how impactful that would be, but looking back, it was the best thing I could've done to calm my fears and believe in myself. I was able to track my progress, so even the smallest accomplishment motivated me to keep going. Things seem more attainable when you chip away at them one piece at a time. It also helps to celebrate small victories.

In addition to my diary, I had a wall calendar of tennis star, Andre Agassi, that I wrote on everyday. I made notes about the events going on, at my school and his, to see how many opportunities I would have to see him, and when. If 1991 Andre Agassi with his strangely-hot mullet doesn't motivate a boy-crazy 16-year-old girl to find love, I don't know who will. Every night I crossed the days off on the calendar and then looked ahead to the plans for the next day. What would Andre do?

With my goal written in my diary and Andre Agassi as my wingman, I was now accountable for taking action. That accountability was amplified when I started to share my hopes and dreams with friends. After I started telling a few friends that I wanted to go to the Vice Versa Dance with Brian, the word seemed to spread pretty quickly. For a girl who was ordinary and working hard to blend in, it felt like everyone knew within just a few days. At that point, I really didn't have an option of giving up because then everyone would know that I failed. I didn't know how many people actually knew about my crush, but the thought of it was unsettling. That feeling definitely fueled me even more because I wasn't sure which would be harder to own up to, being too afraid to ask him or having him say "no" when I did. For all I knew, Brian already heard that I was on a mission to ask him to the Vice Versa Dance. The thought of that definitely kept me focused and terrified at the same time.

That same feeling of accountability is what kept me focused after high school and beyond. Whether it was to get a date or to find a job, setting attainable goals is what led to my success in all aspects of my life. I've been experimenting and researching the different ways to use goal setting for decades. It's these projects that led me to developing my own goal-setting guide. If you would like a copy of my "I Need A Goal Workshop" guide that I use to help people go after everything they want in life, please send me an email at Tracie@HitzAndBranding.com. Be sure to include some information about a goal you achieved, as well as one where you fell short so I can provide some additional insight into this critical step that takes some of the risk out of taking action.

CHAPTER FIVE

DATING IS ADVERTISING

As I thought about that Vice Versa Dance deadline, I started to calculate a plan. A plan that I realized years later was actually a marketing plan. Back in the 90s, it was thought to take a consumer seven times hearing an ad before they would take action. The thought of making contact with Brian seven times made me nauseous. It would be so much easier if one quick conversation would end in getting a date. But even today, the impact of advertising rarely happens that quickly.

Back in high school, there were fewer ways to reach people, so we weren't engaging regularly like students are now. Because of this, the efforts I made were pretty deliberate. This amplified the importance of every encounter because they were few and far between. I wasn't able to drop a quick email, send a funny text, or post an amazingly fun picture on social media. If I wanted Brian to know that I was funny and ambitious, I had to tight roll my favorite jeans, tease my hair, and jump into my freshly painted Mustang in hopes that he would be where I was headed. If did run into him, I had to be quick on my feet to say something funny during the short amount of time we might get together. We would most likely be standing in a large group if we were together, so every word I said could be heard by the masses. The masses that probably knew that everything I was doing was in hopes of getting a date to the Vice Versa Dance. It was a lot to process at such a young age. Accountability can be stressful, but the more prepared you are, the easier it is to push through it.

In high school, my plan could be broken down into three advertising mediums*, which means if I wanted Brian to hear my message, I needed to hit these avenues multiple times. Without actually knowing that seven was the number of times that I should be shooting for talking to him, I did quite a few more than that during the six-month timeframe.

IN PERSON
Thankfully, he was active in sports and we had mutual friends so that made it a little easier to cross paths with him. Even though he didn't play football, he was a member of the chain gang on the sidelines that handled the signal poles for the game officials, so he was at every home football game in the fall. When it switched to basketball season, it was easy to justify going to the home and away games because my friends who attended his school were going too. There were usually opportunities to see each other for

a minute or two after the games.

WORD OF MOUTH
While it was a little unsettling not knowing how many people knew about my goal, their testimonials about why they thought I was someone he should get to know were the key to my success. Their endorsements were like great Amazon reviews because reviews are what help take the risk out of buying the product. When the consumer knows that other people are happy with their purchase, they are more likely to try it. When the words come from someone you know, it's even more impactful. The trick is making sure that what they say is positive and truly represents who you are. False advertising doesn't work in business and it definitely doesn't work in dating.

TELEPHONE
As I mentioned, it was likely that his mom would answer the main landline when I called. It was also very possible that he didn't have a phone in his bedroom so once I got the nerve to make the phone call and talk to his mom, the conversation might then be heard by his entire family. That shyness that plagued me growing up was the reason that the telephone wasn't my favorite option. I reserved this one for emergencies only.

* DIRECT MAIL
A fourth possible medium, if we had gone to the same school, might have been exchanging notes in the hallway. I loved doing this everyday with my best friends at my own school because I just couldn't wait

a few hours to tell them about what I had for lunch or what my teacher said in Spanish class. This is probably why I love texting so much now. It reminds me of the fun of passing notes back in the day. As embarrassing as those notes are to read decades later, it would've been great to use this avenue as a way to chip away at my Vice Versa Dance goal. This would've been the medium that felt the most comfortable to me.

Only having three mediums kept things simple but still diverse enough to have a good mix of communication. Everyone takes in information differently so I had to figure out which of these methods would work best for both of us. What I found was that word of mouth was the most effective way of reaching him because it was so frequent. With so many people talking to him about me, I was starting to get into his head. Of course, not all of these kids were doing sales pitches on why he should date me, but even if they made a quick comment like, "I heard that girl from the Catholic school likes you," it helped my cause. Frequency is huge. It was also effective because he was hearing things that I was way too shy to say myself. For him, he could take in what they were saying and process it later. There wasn't any pressure to respond in the moment, and because of this it seemed like we were both more prepared to talk when we did run into each other later.

If I could do it all over again knowing what I know now, I would've spent more time making sure people understood who I was so they could tell my story. Your story is everything, which is why self-reflection through a SWOT analysis is beneficial in all aspects of your life. Be aware of how people perceive you to make sure it's in line with who you believe you are. This is your brand. This is the messaging that will help when you're looking for a date, a job, a friend, etc. Your brand is everything.

Once you know who you truly are, you can identify the people who will help you grow into who you want to be. This means people who are so alike that you connect on everything, as well as people who are so different they push you beyond what you thought was possible. In high school, I surrounded myself with friends who wanted to be kind and take over the world; so then I targeted a guy who had those same core values. He was a shy, do-gooder filled with ambition just like me. Ambition is one of those values that has gotten even more important to me through the years, but it was a huge factor even in high school. That was what attracted me most to Brian. I knew he would make me better.

CHAPTER SIX

DATING IS PREPARATION

Once you know the traits you value most, you go to the places where you can find those same types of people. As a teenager, study hall was a great place to figure out who was ambitious just by taking a quick glance around the room to see who was actually using the time to study. There weren't many. The guys taking a nap, copying homework, or playing pranks weren't the ones for me. While I love a good laugh, I cringe when it is mean spirited and comes at someone else's expense.

Decades later, I was still looking for places where I could make these types of broad observations in hopes of finding someone who connected with me. Knowing a few key characteristics makes it easier to figure out where they are most likely to be. For example, I like guys who are interested in sports and enjoy being in the middle of the action, so I went to sporting events and sports bars to find them. If health and nutrition are important to you, join a gym or a running club to meet someone with that same value. If you love to throw dinner parties, take a cooking class to see who else might be in there. Think about where the type of people you want to meet will be. Then, go there. Frequently. When you're there, talk to people. That last part doesn't sound that hard, but it's actually one of the most difficult things to do. You can't just show up. You have to engage.

It's difficult because we don't take the same time to prepare for meeting new people as we would for other things in our lives, like a presentation or a job interview. We are ready to put our best foot forward in all of those scenarios, from anticipating interview questions to choosing our clothing to memorizing the key points in the presentation. Think about the preparation you put into your last job interview to then take some of those same things into consideration when you're faced with a situation where you are meeting someone new. For example, picking out the best outfit, having stories ready that show your strengths and experience, preparing questions to ask, sending your resume to someone for review, and reaching out to your references for support. The actions you take to advance in your career can also help you move forward in dating.

Every time I thought there was even a slight chance I might run into Brian, I took the time to look my best. Thank goodness for those bottles of Aqua Net hairspray to make sure my big hair didn't fall. I would also be prepared with a few stories to make sure I was able to keep the conversation going. If the conversation ended, I lost that precious time I needed to tell my story. I would also be constantly evaluating what was working and what needed to be improved after every conversation. That went from the topics we covered that seemed to be of interest to the amount of time I was talking in general. While I was shy, he was even quieter, so I made a conscious effort to make sure I wasn't dominating the conversation.

I was always ready to pivot to another story or ask him a question that he would be excited to answer. For those questions, I could ask him anything about baseball and he would light up talking about it, so I was sure to have some baseball stories of my own to share to build that connection. He was (and definitely still is) a huge St. Louis Cardinals fan, and at the time I was too. Growing up in Central Illinois, that area was split down the middle between the Cubs and the Cardinals. Despite my mom's best efforts, I cheered for the Cardinals because they were winning, my aunt and cousin were fans, and Ozzie Smith was pretty much the coolest player out there because he did backflips onto the field. While Brian was a super fan down to keeping score and memorizing stats, throwing out these little tidbits of info got his attention if the conversation needed a boost.

Once I had a good grasp on what to talk about, I worked on the best way to actually talk to him. The phone was terrifying, so even though we fidgeted, struggled making eye contact, and appeared to be all-around awkward, spending time in person was still the best fit for us. This shyness would only be amplified over the phone because we couldn't see those nervous smiles that encouraged us to keep talking. It was tougher to power through the awkward silences when we were on the phone. I saw the phone as being a very serious move because making a phone call was intentional. So while I was extremely intentional when running into him at these events, the perception was that these were actually casual encounters. That seemed to take some of the pressure off on both sides even if he was starting to figure out that I didn't leave much to fate.

Even now the phone isn't my preferred method of communication. On my birthday, I will get tons of messages via text and social media, but only two voicemails from my parents (Cubs fans) and my aunt and uncle (Cardinals fans). I rarely even hear my phone ring, hence the reason they have to leave voicemails on my birthday. On the off chance I actually make a call, people always answer because they assume it's an emergency. They think I must be dying. Sometimes they sound disappointed when they realize I'm just calling to ask a completely ridiculous question. Being on the same page to communicate helps build a relationship because it puts you more at ease in what can sometimes be a stressful situation. Knowing the right communication method is just as important as being prepared for the actual conversation.

When you're not actually involved in the conversation, be sure to prep those who are. With word of mouth being so important for me in high school, I had to make sure these people had the best information about me. For my close friends, they already knew me well enough to spread my message and it was easy to update them on my life so they were ready with any new tidbits worth sharing. For those kids I didn't know as well, I was intentional about the stories I shared with them. I was sure not to tell the one where I tripped in the cafeteria nearly spilling my chicken sandwich with mashed potatoes and gravy. I made sure they knew about the funny thing that happened on the way to doing my service hours or the latest random story about a mishap with my old Mustang. Like the times I had to jump-start my car because the alternator was spotty.

Preparing them with the stories that I knew embodied me was the best way that they could help me with my marketing plan. Perception is reality so I was hoping what they saw was a nice, funny girl who loves sports and wants to change the world. I didn't want them to just talk about how much I liked this guy. I needed them talking about something of substance so he was learning more about me with every conversation no matter how short. I didn't want them to scare him away by constantly telling him that I had a huge crush just because they had nothing else to say.

I also hoped there were enough positive kids sharing my message to counteract anything negative that may be said. It wouldn't be high school if there weren't mean girls. I wanted to be prepared for anything, and the best way to do that was to be constantly monitoring the situation. Take note of what is working, especially the message you are sharing and the way it is being perceived. Find the ways that work best to communicate for you and the other person, and make sure you are consistently reaching them those ways. Adapt the plan as necessary.

CHAPTER SEVEN

DATING IS STORYTELLING

At the core of the plan is the story, that unique one that each of us has to tell. Once you know that story, you need to figure out how to tell it with all of the characters that come in and out of your life. Mean girls and all. The characters in the story are crucial, especially the main character and how he/she responds to whatever is thrown at them. How do YOU respond?

A character is a collection of qualities. These are what make up who you are. The qualities guide the story, so they need to come together in an interesting way so you don't lose the reader. When you tell a story, every word should contribute to building a connection. It's okay if not everyone feels something when they hear your story. We've all had a friend rave about a book or a movie, and then we read it or watch it and don't feel the same way. I've been set up on blind dates where my friends said they had the perfect guy for me only to find out the reason they set us up was because we were both single. That was it. No other reason. We can't let these missed connections hold us back or make us doubt who we are. Your character is strong because it is so uniquely you.

The characters I hung around with in high school were a lot like me, so we stayed out of trouble but still managed to find ourselves among some of the cool kids at the other high school. Being good at sports tends to do that. To be clear, I was not the one who was good at sports, but my friends were. Brian absolutely dominated them. That was the core of our story plot. He wasn't like most of the other guys on the team, but there's a bond between teammates, especially when they are really good. Brian even got the attention of the popular girls because they connected to that part of his story, but it never went anywhere because they didn't connect with everything else about him.

The more time I spent with him, the more I connected with him. Nice, dorky, and ambitious were some of the qualities that made up both of our characters, so I stayed true to myself by sharing things with him that others didn't really understand. Like, my love of woodworking or my appreciation for a really good pun. I was always prepared with random facts to get a conversation started even if I poked fun at myself. Like being one of the first 600 members in the New Kids on the Block Fan Club. The more random the fact, the more entertaining the conversation. Because our conversations were fun, it became easier to have them, and then they became more frequent. And don't forget that frequency is a key to marketing.

I went to his basketball games in hopes of getting a few minutes with him after the game. Sometimes my friends and I would join the crowd of kids cruising up and down Main Street on a random weekend night just to see if he was there. If we didn't see him, we might take a quick detour by his house to see if he was home. If he was, we usually went home too. No sense in wasting our time on something we didn't enjoy, especially when it wasn't going to get me closer to my goal. It was because of these brief encounters that this goody goody decided to sneak into a postgame event at his high school. It was that night that I knew he was starting to connect with me. Dorky ol' me. When he walked across the floor, he gave me a world of hope with just that one word.

"Dance?"

That's the word that I saw everyday in my journal. It's what I had been working towards all these months. All of the time and energy I put into telling my story was actually working. The risk I took putting myself out there to him, and to what felt like the entire high school, was paying off. This marketing process was helping to build my confidence to finally ask him to the Vice Versa Dance. I ran through all of the encounters in my head as a way to reassure myself that he might like me. Even those moments on the dance floor where we barely spoke during the Journey and REO Speedwagon songs made me believe that it wasn't crazy to think that he could say yes. But I was still extremely nervous to ask.

Because of these nerves, I decided to ask him over the phone. It would add another level of anxiousness knowing his mom would probably answer, but this felt like my best option because I figured that if he said, "no", I could quickly hang up and pretend like nothing ever happened. The thought of being rejected in person was too much for my 16-year-old brain to handle. It was a vision I was sure would be stuck in my head for years to come. With everything I learned over the last few months, I went with the phone call in hopes that it would make the whole experience less traumatizing.

Once that decision was made, there was still a little more planning necessary for this quick phone call. First, I tried to pick the date and time of the call based on the best chance that he would be the one to answer. With what I knew about his schedule, I went with a weeknight after practice, but before dinner in hopes that his mom either wasn't home yet or would be busy fixing dinner. I thought about driving by his house to see if he was home because the thought of leaving a message with his mom was terrifying. That's how nervous I was! But that seemed a little extreme since we lived 20 miles apart. I was just looking for an excuse to delay making the call. Excuses hold us back. They keep us in that safe place. We start to believe in these excuses. We find comfort in these excuses. Doing nothing is easy.

Next, I had to prepare for all possible scenarios.

1) What if his mom answered the phone and he was home?

2) What if his mom answered the phone and he wasn't home?

3) What if he answered the phone?

I jotted down one set of notes for what I was going to say if he was home and another set of notecards if he wasn't. The notes included an outline to keep me on point in case my nerves made it impossible to focus. This was a pivotal moment in our story, so being prepared was essential.

BULLET POINTS 1 & 2
My outline started with the introduction where I asked what he was doing because I wanted to make sure I had his full attention. If he was in the middle of something or getting ready to eat, I didn't want him to jump off the phone before I got the nerve to ask him. The thought of calling him back stressed me out even more.

After confirming that he had time to talk, I gave him a compliment about his basketball game to break the ice a little. He always had a great game, so this was a consistent way to ease into a conversation with him.

BULLET POINTS 3 & 4
Once I felt a little more comfortable, I asked him what he had going on so I could get a feel for whether or not he had time to go to the dance, although I had already checked his basketball schedule to make sure he didn't have a game. I was hoping I would also be able to figure out if he had any interest in going.

Then, I shared a funny story about something I did with two of my closest friends to remind him that we are super fun to hang around. He knew both of my friends, so this allowed me to lay the foundation for the night since we would be going with them to the dance if he accepted my invitation.

BULLET POINT 5
I knew we both loved music, so I asked what he'd been listening to in hopes that this would also set the stage for asking him to the Vice Versa Dance. He

loved Dr. Dre and Snoop Dogg, which didn't set me up as easily as I had hoped for making that transition to the Vice Versa Dance, but I managed. I made a reference to how different those songs were compared to when we danced to Journey and REO Speedwagon, and we laughed.

BULLET POINTS 6 & 7

It was time. This was as good as it was going to get for making the transition to ask him to the Vice Versa Dance. I took a deep breath, but I still spoke so quickly that I blurted out everything that I had planned for the night.

I rushed through the details about my friends going with us, our plan for a nice dinner, that we would pick him up, and more. I don't even remember what else I threw at him. Even though I practiced for this phone call, I completely word vomited on this kid as I asked him to the dance. And then I waited. And waited. For what seemed like ten minutes. But, he said yes! I could barely breathe. I looked at the piece of paper in an effort to speak, but I was out of notes. Why hadn't I written "Say Goodbye" on the notecards?! All I could think to do was hang up. And then I could breathe again. I quickly dialed my best friend, who would be going with me, to tell her that Brian said, "yes". I was shaking with excitement. We giggled and giggled. Then, we started talking about the next part of the plan; actually going to the dance. Oh, good lord.

Deciding to double date with my BFF was something that I didn't even think twice about, but it was one of the smartest things I could've done to continue marketing myself. When she decided to take our friend, Scott, that was a game changer. I would be at ease having two of my closest friends there, but I was also banking on the fact that Scott would have us all laughing the entire night. He was by far my funniest friend, and possibly the sweetest too, so I knew there was no way that we wouldn't have an amazing time with Scott there. It wasn't just about getting the first date, now I had to prepare even more for going on the actual date. I needed these two characters by my side to really tell my story.

This meant a whole night of testimonials. From two people who knew me so well. They could tell stories that made me look nice, funny, and ambitious. I was confident they would paint a great picture of me, but let's not forget that I brought along my funniest friend. Usually your funniest friend gets some laughs from telling stories that might be a little embarrassing, so some of my prep work was making sure Scott knew which stories were appropriate. I didn't want him saying something that would have me crawling under the table in embarrassment. Being a shy teenage girl, I was overly sensitive so that was definitely a possibility. Let's not forget that I painted a car because I was worried that the popular kids at school would make fun of me. However, I felt it was a valid concern because along with "Most Likely To Succeed" and "Class Clown" as part of our Senior Awards, the class also voted on "Best Car" and "Worst Car". That's not what I wanted to be remembered for in high school!

I did as much prep as I could to make sure we had a night to remember, and then I crossed my fingers hoping Scott didn't get so carried away with his story telling that he accidentally let an embarrassing one slip. Despite my best efforts, that's exactly what happened. I don't remember which story it was, as I probably blocked it from my memory, but I absolutely remember my face turning so many shades of red that I was sure Brian could actually feel the heat coming off of it. But he laughed. And not a "wow-you-are-a-weirdo" laughs. It was the most adorable laugh I had ever heard. So I started laughing. It was hard not to with the way Scott can make a funny story so much funnier even when you are part of the punchline. When I started laughing, I saw Scott exhale as he had been holding his breath as soon as he realized that I might explode from embarrassment.

But I couldn't have been happier to have Scott there that night. He helped me tell my authentic story in a way that put me at ease. In fact, he put everyone at ease. Sharing the good stories with the embarrassing ones was refreshing. Eventually the truth comes out, so it was actually kind of fun to show so many different sides of myself on that first date. Even that snort that comes along with my laugh sometimes. The snort that came out so many times that night. We had the most amazing time. Everything was absolutely perfect, right down to my oversized sweater and flowered skort, yes shorts that look like a skirt, along with his multi-colored silk shirt that will never be forgotten thanks to that first photo together at the Vice Versa Dance.

It would be a happy ending to say that we went on to become a couple from that moment, but I can't. Yet. Just like in most stories, there was a "conflict". While he said he had great time and would like to go out again, he also shared that a girl from his school asked him to their Vice Versa Dance the next weekend. Not just any girl. A younger girl … a sophomore! A cute blonde who was known to hang out with older guys. When I started asking around about her, as I'm sure you knew I would do, the things I heard about her made us sound like complete opposites.

I wasn't sure what to think. Or to do. I felt helpless. But it turns out, being completely different actually was a good thing. I learned that making a decision between two things that are similar can be challenging because they can both seem like a good fit. Like when I make those tough choices between a Snickers or a Milky Way. But if I'm trying to decide between a candy bar and potato chips, it's much easier because they are so different. Another life lesson learned through candy.

After Brian told me about his date, I wanted to eat all of the candy bars! I was pretty devastated, but I told him to have fun and to call me if he wanted to hang out again. I really didn't know what else to do. I wanted him to remember me as the fun girl from our date when it came time to decide between salty and sweet. So I waited. Seven long days between my Vice Versa Dance and the Vice Versa Dance he was going to at his own school. We talked on the phone once that week so I wouldn't lose any of the momentum we had coming out of our date. I needed to keep that frequency up if I was going to go head-to-head with my competitor.

While I waited, I analyzed every part of our Vice Versa date over and over. I had prepped myself and my friends for the stories we wanted to tell that night. We shared funny memories and made new ones. I made an effort to learn more about him by asking good questions. Being a writer for the school newspaper and yearbook, I had gotten better at asking open-ended questions and truly listening to the response so I could use that information to ask another relevant question. While I didn't bring notecards on the date, I did prepare questions where I had a fun story to share too, so if he were to ask the question to me in return, I would seem like the most interesting girl in the world. This not only allowed me to get to know more about him, but I was able to share some of my favorite things by setting myself up with these questions. For shy people it's almost second nature to answer the question and then ask the person that same question back, so it worked out perfectly. Even the most self-absorbed people are still likely to ask you the same questions back that you asked them. As I continued to breakdown the date in my head, I felt confident that there wasn't anything else I could've done to make him like me. All I could do now was hope the other girl didn't put in the same extensive prep that I did for a date with Brian.

On the night of his school's Vice Versa Dance my stomach was in knots, so I spent the night at my BFF's house freaking out about what was happening on their date. She didn't live far from Brian, so around 11 p.m. we jumped into her car to take a quick lap by his house to see if he was home. Even though it was the Vice Versa Dance where the girl asks the guy, he was out with a sophomore who didn't have her license so we knew he drove that night. My BFF and I decided that if he wasn't home by 11 p.m., he must have been having the time of his life with this younger girl. Even though we had no basis for the 11 p.m. deadline we made up, I was devastated that his car wasn't there when we drove by. We went back home and rationalized that her curfew was probably 11 p.m. and that's why he wasn't home yet. We updated this random deadline to midnight and took one more lap around his house, and his car was there! Even though this meant absolutely nothing, I felt so much better.

He called me the next day and I held my breath as I waited to hear who he picked. He said he didn't have as much fun on that date as he did with me. Go on! They didn't have much in common, so the conversation was minimal. Go on! He said that he kept thinking about how much fun he had with me (and Scott I'm sure) the weekend before. I couldn't believe it. I won! I won! I won! This had to be how Agassi felt after winning a grand slam tennis title. I was on top of the world. All of the work that went into my marketing plan paid off. Despite the conflict that popped into the story, we had a resolution that gave me the ending I was hoping for when I set that goal to "Dance" six months earlier.

CHAPTER EIGHT

DATING IS BEING INTERESTING

As I look back now to that Vice Versa "Dance Off" between me and the sophomore girl, I wonder if things would've ended differently if she had prepared more for the date? If she had done any research she would know that despite being an athlete, he's actually very shy. She shouldn't have assumed that he would dominate the conversation like other people she dated. Having some conversation topics ready may sound like it takes the fun out of the date, but doing this is actually what makes the date fun. Maybe she didn't pitch herself on the date because she never had to do that in the past. She was young and pretty so I get it, but she would've had a better shot if she had been ready to tell her story. Or maybe she did share everything she wanted to with Brian, but he just didn't connect to it. As a 16-year-old girl, I didn't care about any of that. I was just excited that he picked me! That he connected with me.

I saw pictures of them from the dance and this girl definitely had her packaging together that night. She was way more stylish than me, so she would've made this a harder decision for Brian if she had taken that same amount of time working on what she was going to share with him on the date. Packaging plays a big part in a consumer's choice. When I'm walking down the candy aisle, I never know what will catch my eye. Sometimes I'm drawn to the candy that has the bright packaging, but then when I read the ingredients, I might decide not to buy it. That's similar to your packaging when you're trying to get someone's attention. I spent a lot of time picking out my outfit and doing my hair for the Vice Versa Dance, but I know if you put me next to the sophomore, it would've been two totally different choices. My big sweater was no match for her tight-fitting dress. I could only hope that once he looked past the initial packaging, the details he learned about me would be what he wanted.

When your packaging doesn't match what's inside, you risk losing the trust of the consumer. It's like a company that guarantees rapid weight loss on its product packaging, but doesn't deliver on the results. Consumers won't purchase that product again because the company lost their trust. Staying true to your story includes your packaging since that's the first thing people will see. Use this as another tool in your marketing plan to tell your story. Does what you're wearing right now reflect the person you are?

Once you catch someone's eye, you need to keep his or her interest. Everyone is interesting; they just aren't interesting to everyone. The challenge in sales is finding the people who resonate with your product. If you don't know what makes you interesting, then take the time to figure it out. I know you have a unique story to tell! Define the qualities that make up your character. Your SWOT analysis is a great place to start. In addition to that self reflection, take a minute to ask yourself questions like the ones I look to whenever I'm evaluating where I'm at in life. Add your own questions that will help you adjust as you continue to grow.

Dating Is Being Interesting

- What drives you?
- What are you most proud of?
- What makes you happy?
- What triggers you?
- What makes you excited to get up in the morning?

Even as a 16-year-old girl from a small town in Illinois, I had a story that was interesting to some people along the way. The more I shared the moments that I was proud of (e.g. woodworking champion, perfect attendance, painting my car), the more stories I realized that I had to share. I didn't know it then, but when I was putting together the notecards for that Vice Versa Dance phone call, that's exactly what I was doing. I was preparing to be interesting. If you were going to ask someone out right now, what moments would you jot down on your notecard? Which of those moments have gotten the best reactions when you've shared those stories?

I wasn't interesting to most people in high school, but that didn't keep me from looking for people who would connect with my story. I'm glad I got the courage up to take a chance on asking Brian to the Vice Versa Dance because that experience was another lesson in how to get what you want in life. Brian and I went on to date for the rest of high school and into our freshman year of college. We found each other interesting, and funny, and dorky, and all of the other things that allowed us to grow together. I'm proud of the two ambitious kids we were and how hard we worked to go after our dreams; me of being a writer for *Sports Illustrated* and Brian working to be a professional baseball player. It was special when those two dreams intersected over the summer when one of my biggest feature stories for our hometown newspaper was about the success Brian was having as a college baseball player.

It was an important time in our lives to have someone who is supportive and lifts you up as you learn. This love story is something that I will always cherish because it showed me who I can be with someone else without losing who I am at the core. The bar was set high from my very first love, so when people ask me how I can still be so positive when I've been dating for over 25 years, it can be summed up in one word.

Dance.

A gift for you

Hi, Enjoy your gift! From Delinda and Marc Rood

amazon Gift Receipt

Send a Thank You Note

You can learn more about your gift or start a return here too.

Scan using the Amazon app or visit **http://a.co/5nFK1R9**

As. Calculated: A Dating Plan So Easy A Teenager Can Do It
Order ID: 114-6017474-0097827   Ordered on January 31, 2019

CHAPTER NINE

DATING IS TIMING

Life truly is a dance, especially when you have the right person by your side. However, even with the most amazing support, a relationship can end because your goals shifted as you were growing. While Brian's dream of having a family never wavered, my time away at college made me realize that I wanted to experience big things outside of the small town bubble I lived in all my life. I wanted to be a writer who had amazing stories to tell. I wanted to be interesting to even more people. Along the way of adapting my goals, getting married and having kids were no longer on my list of priorities. Like, not even in the Top 10. With our goals so far off from each other, we were no longer moving along together so these two ambitious kids grew apart.

Having different goals at any point in the relationship, even from the first message you send, can throw you off track. Timing is everything, so continue to take a step back to see your bigger picture so you know the type of person you need in your life at that moment. Usually, I update my SWOT whenever I'm contemplating a big life decision, which in the beginning was typically centered around my career. If I met someone who understood that I was obsessed with my job that was a bonus at that time in my life. Finding my husband wasn't my priority. In addition to my full-time job where I worked nights and weekends, I also had up to three part-time jobs. I was all about learning and experiencing everything I could while living in Chicago. Time was precious, but I always found time for the things I loved to do. So that's how I met the guys I dated in my 20s, either at work or when I was out and about exploring the city. While a few of those encounters turned into serious relationships, they all ultimately ended for the same reason as my high school relationship: I was dating guys who wanted to settle down. The timing was always off.

A difference as big as getting married and/or having kids is an obvious reason for a relationship not working, but even short-term goals can have that same effect. Not aligning with your goals is what can make dating seem so frustrating. Being on different pages from the start is what contributes to so many people deleting dating apps and swearing they will never go online again. Some even swear off dating for months because they don't want to deal with it. When I hear people tell me they are "taking a break from dating", it's usually because they want the other person to be more proactive, move faster, and not run from commitment, which are all signs that you don't have the same goals. If you aren't going to the same place, it's hard to move at the same speed, and that can be frustrating. If you decided to use a dating app because you want to find a boyfriend/girlfriend, but the men/women you meet just want a distraction from their last relationship, you are setting yourself up for heartbreak. Even if you have an amazing connection on that first date, it's challenging to turn that into something more because you aren't going after the same thing. Trust me on this! More on that later.

Checking in with yourself frequently helps to figure out what you really want in a partner. When you're prepared with that information, it can push the other person to share what they're looking for too. Honest conversations aren't easy, especially with people you don't know very well, but they save time, frustration, money, and heartbreak in the long run. You don't always need to have that serious "we need to talk" conversation. Often times, the other person shares the information in pieces if you are listening for it. Even though most dating advice warns against sharing information about your past relationships on the first few dates, people almost always do. This is where you can get a glimpse into the things from their past that are affecting their actions today.

When your date says things like, "this is moving too fast" or "'I'm not looking for anything serious", there is something from their past that may be holding them back from moving forward with you. If you think there might be a future with this someone who seems to be keeping their distance, try to be patient as you ask questions that can help you get the real story before giving up on them. Listen to what they are saying, but also look for the meaning behind it. There is always more to the story if you take the time to look for it. This also goes for listening to yourself and being honest with yourself when you do your own self-assessments. Make sure you are being true to who you are right now so you aren't projecting your past relationships onto the current situation. We spend a lot of time dwelling on the past and/or looking ahead to the future, but living in the present is where you start to go after everything you want in life.

CHAPTER TEN

DATING IS MARKETING

Living in the present means adapting from what used to be and embracing all of the things in front of you. Get excited about more opportunities! Moving from only a few avenues available to find a date in the '90s to decades later where there are endless ways people can connect can seem overwhelming, but it was actually pretty amazing. I was able to explore and experiment as I crafted an effective marketing plan that landed me over 175 dates in eight years. Once I figured out what fit my personality I just kept up the repetition so I was consistently getting out there.

Approaching these avenues with a marketing mind is what kept me focused and on track, so to show you just how simple these marketing principles are, I've picked out some of my favorite marketing advice. I started using this advice to guide me in my career, but then I found success in dating.

TELL A TRUE STORY

In order to genuinely connect with people, you need to be true to yourself even if that means you won't appeal to someone you are attracted to. Being rejected is actually a good thing! It saves that time, frustration, money, and heartbreak I keep talking about because eventually you will reveal your true self so it's easier to just put everything out there at the beginning. Be proud of who you are!

When I attended a speed dating event years ago, we had six minutes with each of the guys that day to tell them everything we possibly could so we could decide if we wanted to spend more time together. In theory, we had three minutes each to tell our story. Speed dating can be an awkward situation for sure, especially with the other person taking notes while you talk. If you've never been to a speed dating event, the organizers encourage participants to take notes so they can remember the highlights from each conversation since so many people shuffle through in a short amount of time. So once you look past the note taking, you concentrate on talking about yourself for those three minutes. If you're prepared, the time flies by, but if you're not, it can be some of the most awkward minutes you've ever experienced in your life. Prepare those random facts and stories that make you interesting to see how the other person reacts. Don't spend the time on the ordinary. If those three minutes are dragging on, then you take note to then reset for the next person. Don't get discouraged. If you are taking notes during the event, try to be subtle, unlike the guy who crossed my name of his list while I was still sitting at the table.

The first few guys at the speeding event were so nervous that they needed me to get the conversation started. I preferred this because I hoped I could help them feel at ease since my years of practice had calmed my nerves in these situations. That shy girl from high school was long gone. I always came to play! I was fully prepared to talk about myself for days. I could talk to a wall at this point in my life.

Then, the final guy of the night sat down in front of me. He was dressed in a three-piece suit complete with a pretty sharp pink pocket square. He definitely had his packaging together. I barely had a chance to introduce myself before he started in on his prepared pitch, which he said in a complete monotone voice as if he was just trying to get through these last six minutes of the day. He was noticeably exhausted and frustrated at this point. He powered through his speech where he told me that he is divorced, has a daughter who likes gummy bears, goes to church twice a week, doesn't drink, wants more kids, and isn't a child molester. He finally took a breath after that last little nugget of info, which was not any sort of joke, so I jumped in to find out more. Good or bad, he was now interesting to me.

"Not a child molester? Just curious as to if that question comes up a lot at these events?"

"You'd be surprised what some of these women want to know, so I want to make sure I'm putting everything out there," he said. "This is me."

Then, he went right back into his prepared pitch,

checking his watch constantly so he could finish within his allotted time so that I could have mine. I didn't need all three of those minutes to know that he wasn't for me, and he also knew within minutes that I wasn't the one for him. I mean, I was holding my second drink of the day during the Sunday event, I hadn't gone to church in a while, and he asked me if I wanted to have kids because he wants to have two more. This conversation did not change my mind about wanting to become a mother. He told his authentic story, including the fact that his mom is the one who keeps signing him up for these events, and I told mine. In the end, it didn't work and that's okay. I learned a lot in those six minutes, and at the event in general. It was a great experience even though I walked away with no matches that day. With his direct approach to dating, and help from his mom, I have to believe that it was only a matter of time before he found exactly who he was looking for in life. He knew what he wanted and he was fully prepared to get it.

IDENTIFY YOUR TARGET MARKET

These are the people who you believe will connect with your values, priorities, and story. They will want to know everything about your character.

For me, that broader target was a single guy who likes sports, which worked out well because I'm always out attending sporting events or going out to the bar to watch games. That is something I already love to do, so it was easy to know where to find them.

What I did to increase my chances of meeting someone was always go out for the biggest sporting events so there are more guys to pick from. I also tried to go to sporting events in the morning and/or afternoon during the week because not many women take off work to watch sports. Besides my girl friends who came with me, there weren't many women out for these big events. I found that my competition was definitely way less on a workday, so I made it a point to never miss these opportunities. Some of my most successful events included Chicago Cubs Opening Day and the first two days of March Madness for the NCAA Men's Basketball Tournament. The guy-to-girl ratio is incredible, which can be not-so-scientifically measured based on how long the men's line was for the restroom while I just walked right into the women's restroom. If you're a woman, that's when you know you are doing something right!

DEFINE YOUR AVATAR

As crazy as dating can be, this has nothing to do with aliens. An avatar is the concepts and philosophies that embody someone. In the marketing word, avatar is being used as a term that means defining your ideal consumer. Marketers get very specific about who they want to engage with through their campaigns. In dating, it means identifying who you want to meet so your message can be catered to this type of person. When you are putting together your messaging, imagine you are talking to someone specific. This helps you stay focused on the type of person instead of straying from who you are because you are trying to attract more people. More is not always better. Some marketers even give their avatars a name. Mine is obviously Andre.

I needed to go deeper on my broad target of single guys who like sports. I mean, isn't that most of the world? Getting this narrow might seem like you're going to lessen your chances of finding someone, but if you try to talk to everyone, no one will hear you. For me, finding a guy who likes sports was easy, especially in a sports town like Chicago, so I needed to get into the details of age, personality, religion, and more. Identify any characteristics that will help find the places where your ideal avatar will most likely be. With "doesn't want kids" being one of my key descriptors for my avatar that changed the age range I was looking to date. With that shift in age to 40+, that also changed the places I was going to look for them.

In my early 30s, chatting with the cute guy on 25-cent wing night was fun, but after a few dates, I had honest conversations with myself about what I wanted. One of my favorite young dates was barely 25 years old, playing Xbox with his three roommates until all hours of the night, and always called in sick to work. We were going down two different paths, so even though I "changed" his name to Donald when everyone else called him Donnie, I knew it was never going to work. Even though it seemed crazy to let go of someone I enjoyed being with, when I forced myself to be honest about who my avatar is, I had to let some of these guys go. I didn't want to miss out on meeting someone else because I was investing my time in a guy that I knew wasn't for me. As a single woman in her mid-30s, that wasn't always easy, but it saved that time, money, and energy that is important to me because it would've ended eventually.

STOP MASS MARKETING

Mass marketing is dead. When you try to be all things to all people, you end up talking to no one. Just like this book. I want to help everyone find the love of his or her life, but I know that my process isn't for everyone. I didn't compromise my beliefs to try to write a book that would appeal to everyone. I focused in on YOU. You are the person I want to connect with on a much deeper level.

Getting specific also applies to your marketing plan, not just your avatar. When you walk into a room, you don't jump on a microphone to get everyone's attention. You talk with small groups and individuals to figure out who connects with you. Trying to talk to the masses no longer works in marketing, and it doesn't usually work in dating. That's why companies are tracking everything we do, so they can craft the perfect message about the perfect product for the people who are most likely to respond to it. And it works!

The first thing I always do to cut down the crowd to a smaller pool is figure out who is single. Thank you wedding rings! These are obviously very helpful for identifying the married folk, but more calculated measures are needed to figure out who is completely unattached. I thought about what Godin would do. He's my idol. He is a marketing genius who teaches about being authentic, remarkable, and targeted. I read his books first to help me in my career, but later on I realized that I was using this same advice in my dating life. Seriously. If you grab any one of his books and read it with dating in mind, you can use these same concepts to get a date. I know this because I've done it. Multiple times. He was the inspiration behind my "Buy 'Em a Beer" tactic that weeded out the single people every time. When I was at a bar, most likely watching sports, I would find a table of guys that appeared to fit my avatar and then ask their waitress if she would take a few beers over to the table. She was instructed to tell them that the beer company was running a promotion where single people receive one free beer. This allowed me to narrow a large table full of guys down to three or four potential connections.

CRAFT YOUR ELEVATOR PITCH

Once you have your avatar in sight, this is where your elevator pitch comes in. You need to have the most interesting things about you all ready to be shared in a fascinating way in one minute or less. Similar to the speed dating guy with all of his prepared facts, you can create an elevator pitch, but with a little more emphasis on the story telling. Try to be as engaging as possible when you're doing the pitch so you can draw them into the conversation quickly.

From years of practice giving my elevator speech, I knew the fact that I worked in sports was almost always the hook that got guys interested, especially when I was in a sports bar. I was always ready to weave that into every conversation, and they made it easy on me when they wore a baseball hat with their favorite team. For the "Buy 'Em A Beer" tactic, it was March Madness so I surveyed the basketball games playing on the TVs to find a school that I had a personal connection with and/or had an experience to share. Working at a Big Ten school for 13 years lent itself well to being able to chat about something that happened at any of those conference games that season. Once I had my stories all set, I looked for the guys who were wearing the fan gear of those teams.

There is a fine line between cool and obnoxious when telling a story that involves some behind-the-scenes knowledge of a sporting event so I was always conscious of that when I talked to strangers. Once I had the story set in my mind, as well as a back-up one just in case, I would grab a beer, take a deep breath, and walk over to the table. My opening line was always the same.

"Hey, guys! Isn't it great that single people get free beer today? Just another reason being single is awesome."

I would raise my beer to cheers the guys who also had a beer so they knew that I was single too. Because I was interrupting their group during a jam-packed day of basketball games, I kept my opening line short so I was the least intrusive as possible. If they were interested, I would stick around to chat a little more. I found the most success when I waited for halftime and/or for a game that was a complete blowout.

QUIET YOUR INNER MEAN GIRL

Male or female, our inner mean girl is what attacks our self-confidence just like mean girls in high school. Godin calls it our Lizard Brain and says it is the reason we are afraid. It's what can hold us back from going after what we want in life. Even with a solid plan in place, we can be too scared to execute it. Too scared to take a risk. We must ignore our Lizard Brain.

The first time I asked a waitress to put four beers on my tab to take over to a table of strangers, she looked at me like I was crazy. And rightfully so. I quieted my inner mean girl, but I realized that sometimes I even needed to quiet someone else's. At that point, I could've chosen to believe that maybe my idea was crazy, so crazy that I shouldn't do it. I could've let that inner voice convince me to walk away. But instead, I just asked a different waitress to help me. The second waitress thought it was hilarious, which made everything a lot more fun.

Sometimes I would team up with a friend as my wingwoman, which also helped quiet those doubts. After doing the "Buy 'Em a Beer" tactic several times it was way easier to quiet that inner voice because things always get easier with practice. We all get better with practice regardless of what the activity is. When I got to the table, I was prepared with my elevator pitch, evaluated how things went after I talked with them, made any necessary changes, and got back out there to do it all over again. Because I defined my ideal avatar so specifically, I wasn't surprised that I was rejected along the way. A lot. I told my story and just waited to see who wanted to know more. Sometimes that was no one. Of course that hurt, but when you view rejection as a way to get better, it makes everything hurt less. Even practicing rejection makes you better at it.

I was proud of the progress I was making towards the goal I set to get a date, so I never felt like talking to strangers was a waste of time. Even when I bought the beers, I didn't think it was a waste of money because I was having fun experimenting and growing through the process. We can learn something from every person we meet even if it's not a great interaction. In fact, I learn the most from the worst dates rather than the ones that go okay. Continuing to chip away is better than making no movement at all. Don't listen to that inner voice. Or that waitress who thinks free beer is crazy.

DONE IS BETTER THAN PERFECT

Or as Godin says, just "ship it". Waiting for perfection is just an excuse. We will never move forward if we wait for something to be perfect before we do it. Instead of tweaking the idea over and over in our heads, we need to implement, evaluate, and adjust. It's okay to fail because every failure is another moment of growth. Failure makes us better.

The first time I implemented the "Buy 'Em a Beer" tactic, I didn't know what to expect. I stumbled on my words and ended up only talking to two of the guys at the table, both of which turned out to have girlfriends. It never crossed my mind that guys would lie just to get a free beer. Duh! It's that goody goody quality that kept me from seeing that as a potential challenge the first time. But I didn't see it coming, so I just made an adjustment on the fly when I went to the next table. Instead of going straight into my elevator pitch assuming they were single when they picked up a free beer, I talked more about the beer promotion until I could get them to confirm that they were available.

CALCULATE THE ROI

Return On Investment. This goes for the time, energy, and money I've been talking about because it all counts when calculating your worth. Most of the time when someone gets frustrated with dating it's because they've wasted time, energy, and/or money, so being more strategic in these investments means that the ROI stays high and your frustration is low.

I chose beer because it was cheaper than buying drinks, but full disclosure, I don't like beer. I actually hate it. I hate beer so much that I've only had 13 in my life. Total. And I can tell you exactly where I was for each and every one of those disgusting drinks, as well as why I was compelled to drink it. But dudes like beer, and it made sense to buy a drink that was almost always on special because it kept my investment low. The waitresses who were intrigued by the "Buy 'Em a Beer" tactic would usually give me a few beers at no cost, which probably wouldn't happen if I were asking for liquor. So sometimes beer is good. Just not to drink.

One of the years during the March Madness games, my friend who works for a beer distributor comped four buckets of beer and lent me his work jacket because he wanted to see me in action. By giving me the beers to distribute, he was suggesting that I cut out the middleman, aka the waitress, because he thought it would be more effective. So I adapted the plan. This meant I was the one telling the guys they would get a free beer if they were single, which was nerve racking at first, but with practice it became easier. Making this adjustment actually increased my success rate, and getting the beers at no cost obviously increased my ROI.

WORK ON KNOW, LIKE, AND TRUST

Consumers buy things from people they know, like, and trust. That's why many people are obsessed with seeing customer reviews on products before they make a purchase. Even if they don't know the people writing the reviews online, if enough people are saying the same thing, a sense of trust is built.

When the waitress brought the beer to the table, the guys didn't even hesitate to grab one because they knew her, they liked her, and they trusted her. Even though I was also giving away free beer, ambushing a table of guys watching basketball in a bar didn't mean I could skip straight to that same trust. Having the official work jacket helped, but not every time. At one of the first tables I went to, the guys peppered me with questions about why the company would be giving away beer, how long had I been working there, why my jacket was way too big, etc. I've never been more exhausted trying to give something away. And that includes the time I was almost trampled at a professional soccer game when I was part of the marketing team giving away trial size bars of soap. Tiny bars of soap! I almost died giving away tiny bars of soap. But this group of guys was not as easily impressed by free beer, and they actually wouldn't take the bottle from me. They broke me down and I finally gave up after this exchange.

"How do we know that you didn't rufi these beers?"

"Because the caps are still sealed."

PROVIDE VALUE

People buy products or services that improve their lives, make them happier, or solve a problem. Essentially they want something that makes their lives better. So during that "Know, Like, and Trust" phase, you share not only who you are, but also why having you in their lives will make it better. They need to hear this messaging multiple times before they start believing it, so if you have opportunities to show them value, you are more likely to make the sale.

It seemed to me that giving away beer would be an easy way to provide that instant value, but the messaging was that the beer company was giving away the product, not me. In this scenario, I was just the messenger and the beer company was getting all the credit, so I wasn't exactly building that trust. Plus, I wasn't being honest by holding a beer that I had no intention of ever drinking. Because of the importance of providing value, this was another area where I took notes to adjust the process. If I wanted the guys to trust me, the truth had to come out before the end of the conversation. And not just the truth about hating beer, but about the fact that I was the one actually running the beer promotion. After chatting for a few minutes with the group, I would zero in on one of the guys who seemed to be the most interested. In our side conversation, I would reveal that I actually bought the beers in an effort to meet fun people. If the guy thought I was insane/desperate/annoying, then he's not the guy for me anyway because random ideas are at the core of who I am. This definitely wouldn't be the craziest thing I would ever do if we started dating. The guy I zeroed in on needed to know all of this during our conversation before I left the table. The guys who thought the "Buy 'Em A Beer" tactic was clever/cute/fun are the ones I would have the best chance connecting with because if we started dating, they would see that this promotion is actually a great representation of who I am at my core.

BE INTERESTING

Everyone has a story that someone wants to hear. Finding that person is the challenge, and that's what can cause frustration when you aren't connecting with someone. Godin says, "be remarkable", and uses the idea of creating a purple cow as an example of standing out among all of the ordinary cows. He illustrates this point by asking the reader what would you do if you saw a purple cow in a pasture? Of course you would be drawn to it because it's unique. It's different. It's interesting.

That is exactly what I was trying to do by approaching these tables full of guys while the other girls chose to stay seated in hopes that the guys would eventually come talk to them. Even though I now straighten my hair and ditched the Aqua Net, I'm still an ordinary-looking girl; so sitting back waiting for guys to talk to me doesn't usually work. Of course, that is the safer play for sure, and works for some. Like my friend who walked into a concert and asked what beer was on tap. The guy next to her turned to tell her about a local beer saw how beautiful she was, and then just handed her both of his beers. She said thank you. He stared. She walked away. He wasn't ready with his elevator pitch, or even his first name, so his free beer tactic didn't work. At all. I asked him what kind of vodka was on tap, but I ended up buying my own drinks that night.

Being interesting is about taking action and taking chances. Even when the guys accused me of putting rufis in their beers, I just let it roll off my back because I was proud of myself for taking action. They didn't find me interesting, and I felt the same, so it was on to the next group to see if we could connect. No big deal. Marketing yourself isn't always the safe move, but it gets results if you can stay focused, brush off rejection, and keep on being interesting. Keep on being you.

Every once in a while, I would be in a sports bar full of people who took off work to watch basketball, and somehow I would stumble upon a guy who doesn't like sports. I didn't even know that was a thing! This would throw me completely off my game because my entire elevator pitch is centered around sports. Sports are a huge part of what makes me interesting, and he didn't care at all. Not even a little bit. My story was not remarkable to him so I tried to pivot the conversation to find something else that we might have in common. Something else that could be interesting to him. Instead of trying to convince him that sports are awesome, I looked for something else to get his attention. When I came up empty, I moved on to the next. He was not my ideal avatar, so there was no sense in wasting time, effort, and money on him. I needed to stay true to finding my Andre.

CUT YOUR LOSSES

Even if you have that time, money, and effort invested in trying to sell yourself to someone, it's okay to give up if it's just not working. Don't keep going down the wrong path. Turn around and start again.

In the case of the "Buy 'Em a Beer" tactic, I usually had about $10 invested in a table, and that's just not worth the time to force my story on people who aren't interested. My time and money would be better spent moving on to another table. If I was able to pivot from sports when the guy wasn't interested, I usually talked about my love of music. I was excited when this resulted in a date, but then during that first date, the connection didn't build. Sure, I loved music, but this guy REALLY loved music. He lost my interest, and I'm sure I had done the same to him. Instead of forcing something just because I had invested some time and money into this guy, I broke it off. It usually only takes one date for me to know if there is a future, which I'm sure sounds hasty, but cutting my losses is one of the reasons my frustration level was so low when I was actively dating.

Sales is a numbers game, so the more people you talk to the more chances you have to meet someone who does connect with you. Don't waste time with those who don't connect. Be intentional. Take action. You can't expect to sit at home every night in hopes that an amazing person will knock on your door to ask you out on a date. Not only is that highly unlikely, but it's also a bit creepy and slightly dangerous for a stranger to actually show up on your doorstep. Please don't answer that door! Unless they have free beer. Then you might want to hear what they have to say, assuming the caps are still on all of the bottles.

INCENTIVIZE THE CUSTOMER

When you take action it often helps to include providing a benefit that makes your offer one that they can't pass up. While it would be great if someone liked you after an amazing elevator pitch, sometimes you need to turn things up a notch.

The free beer gave me the opportunity to have a few minutes with guys who might normally overlook me at the bar, but that time at the table wasn't always enough time to convince them to ask me out. If they did ask for my phone number, I would offer up another incentive to make sure they would actually use it. I would throw out suggestions for a possible event for a first date. Because I was usually in a sports bar, I catered the incentive around a sporting event to give myself the best shot at success. I always found a way to reveal that I worked in sports, so it was easy to slide tickets to an upcoming game into the conversation. Of course, not just any tickets, but great seats to a big game. If I was able to snag some pregame field passes, tailgate passes, or something else that would provide a unique experience, I threw that in too. That had a near perfect success rate for getting a first date, but sometimes it became clear that they only came on the date because of the incredible incentive.

Kudos to them for doing their own ROI assessment figuring that it was worth three hours out of their lives to go with me to an amazing event even if I turned out to be the most boring person on the planet. Sometimes the event itself was just too fun to pass up regardless of who they had to go with in order to get the ticket. Getting them on the date was a great first step, but it was up to me to use that time to share my story. Being able to bring them into my sports world was the perfect way to show them who I was because that is a huge part of my life. Of course, it only worked with those who found my work-obsessed life to be interesting.

So the incentive matters. It's about providing value, but in a way that builds the relationship in hopes that they will know, like, and trust you. Like the guys who went on the date just for the games, there are women who go on the dates just for the free meal even if they have no interest at all in the guy. It happens so much that they've coined terms for it, like "foodie call" and "sneating". Some women have admitted to doing this because they live in an expensive city where they can't afford to experience it on their own. Others find it to be a challenge to see how many free meals they can get each week. Whatever their reasons, they have definitely calculated their ROI on this one.

On the flipside, the guys also calculate the ROI because they are typically the ones paying for the date. So when women complain that the guy they met online is taking too long to move the conversation from messaging to a first date, it could be that he's trying to figure out which dates to go on because there is time and money involved. Some guys only have one free night a week so they put a lot of thought into how they want to spend it. ROI isn't just about money. When they hesitate, sometimes these women become so frustrated waiting on the guys to ask them out that they delete the guys from their phone.

Different goals. Different ROI. Different past experiences. These can all affect whether or not you get a first date. It's not as simple as whether or not he likes you. There is a lot more going into that decision that you probably don't even know about. If I wanted to move things along, I would often take the lead by offering up an inexpensive, quick activity like meeting at the lake to walk the path by the beach.

The time investment is real, and so are the dollars. Some guys are going on two dates a week, which depending on where you live and what you like to do on a first date, it can range anywhere from $30 - $100 per date. That's up to $240 - $800 per month and $2,880 - $9,600 a year. Thousands of dollars a year! These numbers factor into why some of these guys take longer to actually meet up with someone for a date. Knowing that only a handful of these dates might turn into a relationship, this dating numbers game can be quite expensive. For me, when I offered up free tickets to a game it resonated with them not just because it was a cool event and it would save them money, but it showed that I wasn't the girl who expected the guy to pay for everything. It showed that I might also be investing in the possibility of a relationship. If they ran the numbers, the ROI on me could be pretty high so I made sure they knew this about me so they had the info they needed to make their plans for the week. Sales is about eliminating the risk, and that's exactly what I tried to do.

PAINT A PICTURE OF THE FUTURE

Godin says that if you paint a picture of the future, "people will follow". Those who resonate with your story will continue to listen. These are the people you have the best chance of building a relationship with so your focus should turn to them instead of worrying about the larger group of people who didn't connect with it.

Once you have your first dates confirmed, it's time to dig even deeper to see who remains in the mix. The questions you ask and the stories you share will guide the date, so be intentional with your words. People often complain that dates can feel like job interviews because the questions they ask are too personal that early on in a relationship. Like asking someone how much money they make or how long they would wait before moving in with a significant other. Craft questions that help paint the picture but be conscious of what's appropriate for a first date. This time is spent building the relationship to see what resonates over time. Be careful to observe the other person to make note of the right amount of information to share and at what pace you should share it.

In a job interview, it doesn't matter if you are the employer or the job candidate; you both need to figure out by the end of the process whether or not this will be the right fit. Think about the interview questions you typically ask or the questions that resonated with you when looking for a job. Chances are, there are some that can cross over for your first date conversations. My favorite interview questions that helped paint the picture center around ambition, kindness, and teamwork. These are important to me in my career and in my love life, so they are often interchangeable from work to personal. The questions that dig deeper while still keeping things at a good pace actually appear to be specific, but their answers really provide a glimpse into the bigger picture. This helps me get the answers I need without the pressure that comes along with asking extremely personal questions. Crafting questions around your core values is a great way to get people to open up about things that are important to you.

What are you most proud of?
I ask this of every single job candidate regardless of what position I'm hiring because it brings out the most amazing stories. It really gets to the core of who they are, so I make sure I ask this one on first dates too for that very same reason. If they don't have something they are excited to tell me about, then it's doubtful they will be a match personally or professionally.

When you were a child, what did you want to be when you grew up?
When I ask this in an interview setting, it helps me see how fun and creative the job candidates are at their core. When I worked at a Big Ten Conference school

and they answered the question with something like, "I grew up dreaming of becoming a sports marketing professional at a Big Ten school", I was weary that they wouldn't fit into the team dynamic because I wasn't looking for people who only say what they think I want to hear. I want people who are going to speak up, challenge me, and be confident in who they are so we can accomplish amazing things. I want them to see the fun in asking a former NFL player to paint himself purple for a nationally televised football game. I surround myself with people who push me to be better, not nod and agree with me. Crazy ideas are only successful if you've thought them all the way through, so I need those people around me.

I would even provide them with an example of my childhood dream of being Janet Jackson's back-up dancer in hopes that would put them at ease to say whatever their childhood dream was back then too. To take a second to show who they really are. Their true stories. I hoped it would jolt out some fun since that is also an important quality that I want in a teammate, but it didn't always happen. When it does, it can be so telling. Even a common dream of being a professional baseball player can be endearing when they share more of the story behind it. That's what my high school boyfriend wanted to be, and the story behind it made it special. He cherished the time he spent practicing baseball with his dad, as well as valued all of the hard work he put into actually going after the dream. It wasn't just something he thought about as a kid, it was something he actually tried very hard to make happen. And I find that endearing.

What do you enjoy outside of work?

This question during an interview gives me insight into several things, but what I'm looking for is their work ethic. With all of the nights and weekends we work in the sports industry, I want to see if they have a negative attitude. If they start complaining about not having a life, talking about sleeping as much as possible, or telling me about how sad they are that they missed some big events because of work, I know they aren't the right fit for me. I am always looking for someone who works hard, but does it with a smile. I want someone who is flexible and up for anything personally and professionally.

On the dating side, I like this question because ambition is at the core of my being, so I need to be with someone who is full of energy, dreams, and action. If they don't have any interests outside of work, I know they won't want to join me in my jam-packed world. I need someone who can keep up.

Where are your former interns and/or staff members?

This is a question I ask when I'm being interviewed to figure out their leadership style and level of importance that's placed on mentorship. There's not always a respectful way to get information like this when you're the one trying to get the job, so disguising it within an unsuspecting question like this one has worked really well. If they aren't bragging about all the places they've helped people get to, or don't even know what their former staff members are doing now, I get a little anxious to work for people like that.

Helping people makes me happy, so on the dating side, I ask the question more broadly to include younger siblings, people at work, etc. I just want to know how invested they are in helping people in all areas of their lives. I want to know if they are genuinely kind and will make time for those who need them. I want to know if they will be invested in people long term.

After you create your SWOT analysis, you will be able to assemble some great questions of your own that will help you in business and in dating. Look at your strengths and weaknesses to figure out what questions will bring out the information you need to know when trying to decide if this person could be someone to build a life with in the future. As I assembled mine through the years, there were some questions that only worked for weeding people out in the dating process, especially the following questions.

When was the last time you dressed up for Halloween? What was your costume?

I know there is a large contingent of people who have outgrown Halloween, and rightfully so. However, I love Halloween so I like to ask this question to find out what type of fun is hiding inside of them. If they don't dress up, but don't mind if others do, then I know they can probably handle my personality and the random ideas that can pop up at any time. The guys who went on rants about how stupid the holiday is and everything that goes along with it, including the candy, don't usually make the cut. Candy? How can you hate the candy?

One guy told me that he hates Halloween, but that he would still help me brainstorm a funny costume for the party I was going to a few weeks later. That works! I told him that I like to dress up as random people in history, but with a girly twist, like my flirty Amelia Earhart costume the year before. While I appreciated that he was willing to help, his answer had me worried on a several levels.

"You should be sexy Hitler!"

I'm going to Vegas, have you ever been there?
I stumbled upon this question on accident when I was planning a girls' trip to Vegas for my 40th birthday. I was chatting with a few guys on a dating app and the slight mention of going to Vegas resulted in responses that ranged from, "don't forget to go to my favorite strip club" to "you're a fool to be going to Vegas in the Summer". The guy who told me to "have fun and always double down on 11", was the one I continued to talk to after that conversation.

These are the questions that worked for me, so I encourage you to take some time to craft your own that will allow you to be more targeted and strategic so you can save time, money, and energy, which will also keep your frustration to a minimum. When people ask me how I was able to stay so positive throughout 25 years of dating, I tell them that my Dating is Marketing Plan is absolutely the reason. Taking a step back to understand why a guy wasn't asking me out or suddenly stopped messaging helped me to not take things so personally. We all bring our own personalities and experiences into the process, and sometimes those goals just don't match up. It's not personal. Usually. Being able to evaluate the process so I could make adjustments kept me moving forward with a positive attitude. Committing to your goal and to your plan keeps things in perspective. You will see progress, which is always motivating. If you're competitive like me, having a plan makes all the difference in the world for staying focused and positive.

ASSEMBLE YOUR BOARD OF DIRECTORS

I'll say that again. A positive attitude. It's not always easy to stay positive when the most prominent messages you see are negative. There are so many social media accounts that make fun of people they've met and there are blogs dedicated to ripping people apart before and after dates. Even our friends and family can affect our outlook on dating with their negative comments even if they are said out of love. There is a lot of negativity around dating, but if you approach every new person as an opportunity to learn and grow, you can see the good in every situation. You will believe in the process.

It all starts with goals. Setting them and communicating them with your support system, which I call my Personal Board of Directors. These are the people who will do anything for me, including being honest when I'm falling short, starting to lose some of my positive energy, and everything in between. They support me in whatever I chose to do even if it's not the path they would've taken. Some of those members include a colleague turned friend who speaks the truth at all times to everyone, my mom who supports while letting me find my own way, my old boss who sets a bar so high I'm always trying to reach it even though we no longer work together, my brother who wanted so badly for me to find love even though his marriage ended in divorce, a friend ten years younger who never lets me doubt myself, and several amazing wingwomen who are always up for implementing one of my crazy marketing ideas in the dating world.

Having this support is everything. For example, I've never been married, and yet I never dread the holidays because my family doesn't interrogate me about why I haven't settled down yet. That's over 20 Christmases where I could just enjoy time with my family without looking over my shoulder for someone on the hunt to get answers to that burning question.

"Why are you still single?"

Crazy, right?! Not really. My family knows that getting married and having kids wasn't a priority for me, so they weren't surprised if I showed up alone at the holidays. Of course, I'm sure they did a little happy dance the few times I did bring someone home for them to meet, but they kept their excitement to a normal level on the outside. From as long as I can remember, their goal for me was to be happy and they saw evidence of that every single day, so they never felt the need to push me down another path. When everyone is on the same page, it's easy to stay positive and keep plugging away at achieving whatever you want in life.

HAVE FLASH SALES

Something that also makes me happy during the holidays is finding sales. The idea of creating a plan to find the most amazing deal is so fun to me, probably because of that competitive gene I have inside me. Flash sales work to get attention. They drop the price so low that it's hard not to act. Plus, they are only available for a limited time so they can get you to buy on an impulse for fear you will never find something this incredible again.

The ads for these sales communicate exactly what to expect, so there are no surprises along the way, as long as you read the fine print. They are direct and to the point. I wish this were the case in dating. I make it a point to be direct about what I'm feeling because that's the way I would like to be treated. I hope in turn the other person feels comfortable sharing too even if it's going to be a difficult conversation, like telling someone you're just not feeling a connection. Wasting time contributes to frustration, so cutting ties when you know it's not going to work helps to stay focused, which can keep you staying positive. Sometimes when you lay everything out there, it can prompt two people to set up a first date if they had been dragging their feet for a while. Sales prompt action. Setting a deadline gives a sense of urgency. Setting a time limit for taking action often works in dating because you'll get the attention of even the biggest procrastinators this way.

Of course, other times people can get uncomfortable with such a bold move, so they might respond negatively because you've pushed them outside their comfort zone. Sometimes the guy's response will be something rude where he makes it clear that he doesn't care if his window to take action is closing. These types of responses are exactly why more people don't have an open dialogue like this in dating.

People are mean.

Plain and simple. That's the same reason we get nervous to talk to a stranger because we don't know how they will respond, so it's safer to not say anything at all. Waiting seems like the safer play, but it's not the one that prompts action. Not seeing results is what causes frustration. This is an opportunity to take more control of your dating life by creating your marketing plan. Be intentional.

Success in the dating world, and the world in general, would be much more attainable if people were just a little nicer. It's fascinating how the conversation changes when the response is nice instead of mean. When I texted one guy to let him know that I wasn't interested, he responded by telling me that I was too fat to date anyway so he was glad I didn't want to talk to him anymore. I was just trying to save both of us that time, money, and energy that is at such a premium, but he got defensive and that led to a mean comment. A normal reaction on my end would be to fire back a nasty response and then swear off dating apps forever. Instead, this is what I wrote.

"It sounds like you take your workouts very seriously.

Any tips for someone with a bad knee?"

Within minutes he responded with some of his favorite workouts and we messaged back and forth a few times. With some prodding from me, he revealed that his ex-girlfriend broke up with him because he gained weight, so he'd been obsessed with working out since then. He made the comment about weight because a similar comment from an ex-girlfriend hurt him deeply and he wanted me to hurt too. Even though I wasn't the one who said it, my text about moving on triggered something negative from his past. By the end of the exchange, he apologized and I hoped that he learned as much as I did from the situation so that he would handle things differently in the future. Learn from the past, but live in the present.

We are the sum of our experiences, so it's common for people to come into a situation with some triggers that you have no idea are even there. Being a 40-year-old on the dating scene, there was a lot of hurt and distrust out there that came with the people I met, so communication was the key for me to break through in hopes they would see me, not their past. It's not easy to have these deep conversations with people we barely know, but if our messaging is always rooted in kindness, we have a better shot at getting kindness in return. Even though I wasn't planning to date the guy who called me fat, I don't want to end conversations on a negative note with anyone. If someone puts out such a rude response, there is probably a deeper meaning behind it. Let's help people work through their past so we can all enjoy the present while we try to shape our future.

I hope you take away so many things from this book that will help you live the life you want, but at the top of that list is taking the time to see the whole picture. Learning to be confident in who you are, as well as trying to understand those you meet so you can grow together. Even if you only meet for one date and it goes poorly, please leave them with something that can uplift them. We have opportunities everyday to impact people's lives for the better. Choose to be happy. Choose to be kind. Choose to be positive. Even when others aren't. Especially when others aren't. Meeting new people, enjoying great food, and going out on the town should be so much fun. Let's come together to make dating fun again by having kindness at our core.

WRITE A CATCHY SLOGAN

"I wish I was an Oscar Meyer wiener, that is what I truly wish to be."

Oh my, that song has been stuck in my head since I was a kid. Pure marketing genius. Imagine if you created something this memorable in an effort to grab the attention of someone you like.

When I was marketing myself for a date, I wanted to get stuck in people's heads whether they were flipping through online profiles or if we had a conversation at the grocery store. Because some people only look at the photos when dating online, most people don't bother writing anything in their profile. I found that adding a quick "slogan" increased my matches. I had given them a little glimpse into who I was. It brought my pictures to life. This random fact also gave the guys I matched with something interesting to use in starting the conversation besides the way too common, "hey", "sup", and "yo". How much effort they put into that initial greeting was then a great glimpse into their personalities. The sentence that eventually turned into my slogan summed me up pretty well.

"I always get a pedicure on the way to my fantasy football draft."

These thirteen words were able to soften the tomboy vibe that automatically surfaces since so many of my photos involve sports. Adding this text allowed me to show how important sports are to me, but that I also have another side. Being able to start a conversation online about something of interest can build a connection faster than the small talk that usually happens when you first meet someone. When you're competing with other people for attention, having something of interest from the start gives you an edge. Having a slogan is also something that's easy for your friends to share with their single friends when they are trying to set you up on a date. Make things as easy as possible to spread your message. A great place to look for inspiration for your marketing slogan is your elevator pitch, so once you have that together, you will be able to come up with something catchy. Something that is truly you.

PERFECT YOUR PACKAGING

Along with the slogan comes packaging. This is what catches people's eye and sometimes pushes them over the edge to purchase one product over another. Like when I see a fun design for a candy bar. The packaging stands out from the rest and draws me in to learn more about what's inside. If they share the top ingredients boldly on the label, I will continue to dig deeper, like finding the number of calories. I will knock that candy bar back so quickly once I know the calorie count. Putting this type of information out for people to easily see helps you get that initial contact, as well as peaks their interest to learn even more.

One of my favorite dating slogans was inspired by the packaging of a candy bar when my 5'1 friend described herself as "fun sized" in her online profile. She brought this slogan to life through her packaging, which included the clothes she wore in the pictures she featured, the places she picked to take the photos, and the angles that showed she wasn't very tall. This was a great attention getter and a perfect description for this sassy, fun girl. Plus, people seem to be obsessed with height when it comes to online dating, so being shorter than most men was a huge bonus for her when trying to match with them.

Some packaging comes with the job, like men and women in uniform. For the military, this is impactful packaging because we know the reputation that goes along with the people who earn the right to wear those uniforms. Every work uniform usually tells a story. When I see someone in scrubs, I assume that he or she cares about people on a whole other level than me. I mean, I watched all 15 seasons of ER with one had over my eyes. Other people see dollar signs when they pass by a doctor in his coat. While you can't control what people think about the uniform, it usually solicits some sort of emotion so that helps to figure out who might connect with you. I went on a dinner date where the guy was still wearing his scrubs so I assumed he just came from work. I didn't think much of it that he didn't change before meeting me, but by the end of the date he revealed that he didn't even work that day. He just liked wearing them because he usually gets attention whenever he does. He had figured out the importance of his packaging.

Your appearance tells part of your story, so what you wear and what photos you post not only show what you like to do, but what your style is. Your style usually reflects your personality, so take the opportunity to show this by taking the time to pick a great outfit for your photos, your first dates, and every day in between. When I created my online dating profile, I thought about including one of my favorite photos at a sporting event, but it was winter when I took the photo so I was bundled up in so much clothing that you could barely see my face. It also made me look chunky, and I was now aware of how picky people can be about weight! I had dozens of other sports photos that would work just as well, so I picked a different one where you could actually see what I looked like. It turns out that when I changed the photo, I also got more attention because the school in the picture was one that most of the country loves to hate. This photo started several conversations with guys who wanted to know if I went to that school. Evoking thoughts and emotion through your packaging increases the number of people talking to you, as well as the quality of the conversation. Small talk is boring. Be interesting.

When I talk about packaging, it's not about getting dressed up to be someone you're not. I stuck with my big sweater and flower skort even though I knew the other girls were going to have trendier outfits than me at the Vice Versa Dance. You don't need to change your appearance or have professional photos taken for your online profile. Find or take the photos that will show your authentic self without using any words at all. If you always wear your hair in a ponytail or you live your life in leather pants, then make sure that's reflected in your photos. Look through your photos to see which ones make you smile, feel vulnerable, and represent your favorite moments. My photos ranged from sporty to goofy to sweet. For a few weeks, I even included a photo from a wedding where I was a bridesmaid because the picture made me happy. However, I eventually pulled the photo down because that day I was asked to wear makeup for the wedding photos. I never wear makeup. I got a ton of compliments on the photo, but it wasn't me. I wouldn't show up for a date wearing make up, so I didn't want to feature a photo where I had it on.

I've probably worn make up the same number of times that I've drank a beer. I had a traumatizing experience as a sophomore. I wasn't allowed to wear makeup until I was 16 years old, but my friends at school convinced me that for sophomore picture day I just had to wear some blush. Eye shadow. A little lipstick. They picked out an outfit and teased my hair more than usual. I thought making changes to my appearance would make me beautiful. I was very, very wrong. I wore a blazer for picture day! I was uncomfortable in my own skin. I broke the rules my parents set for me by putting on makeup, and I paid the consequences with this photo still living on today. It wasn't me. It was who people wanted me to be.

While the makeup for the wedding was done by a professional, I still felt uncomfortable using that photo because it's not who I am everyday. Or any day really. The pictures you choose for your online dating profile should also be the ones you use for your social media profile pictures. This helps for when your friends set you up on a blind date because the first thing they will do is look for a picture to show that person. Make it as easy as possible on them to find a great one by having the best representation of you as your profile picture. I set people up all the time on blind dates, so I know that when I have to spend a minute or two scrolling through their photos to find a good one, I've now lost some trust because this person sees that I'm struggling to find a photo. They wonder what photos I'm flipping past and why.

Having these real photos posted everywhere, especially on your online dating profile, is part of being targeted in finding your ideal avatar. This might mean fewer matches, but they will be better matches. People will know what to expect when they meet you in person. Managing expectations was definitely the key to my success in online dating. There were no surprises when people met me. Almost every time I met a guy in person after matching online, they would say the same thing.

"Wow, you actually look like your pictures."

So while you may want to crop a photo or use a filter to look better, make sure the photo still shows the real you. Otherwise it makes it harder to build trust on that first date if they feel like you weren't being honest with your photos. When these guys started the conversation with comments about my photos being so real, I asked them how often it happens that people don't look like their pictures. A couple of these guys told me that it happens more often than not. That they've actually left the restaurant without talking to the women they were supposed to meet because they felt like their pictures had tricked them. They were so upset about the false advertising that they didn't even bother to talk to the women.

I had a similar situation when I was meeting up with a guy I met online. He wasn't trying to trick anyone, but the photos he chose made it difficult to tell who he was. I wasn't sure what he looked like because he had four group photos with what seemed like all of the same people in each photo and then one photo of just his dog. I tried to use my detective skills to figure out which person he was in the photo, but I still had my doubts as to what he really looked like. It was obvious that he just tossed up five pictures randomly, so I swiped right on him in hopes that he actually was the guy who I guessed in the photos. When we matched, I agreed to meet with him because he won me over through our conversations. He had me from his first message.

"Hey Tracie. Ok what your favorite place to hang out in the cities you spend time in Nashville? Indy? Chicago?"

Even though I'm a writer who loves grammar, I completely let it slide that he forgot the word "are" in his message because he actually took the time to look at my profile before writing a quick message that was catered specifically for me. It was obvious that he didn't copy and paste a greeting from something he had been sending to other girls. Because of that, we had a great conversation from the start and he continued to ask interesting questions. He actually listened to my answers and seemed engaged in the conversations. It was unlike anyone I had messaged with before. He made me laugh as we continued to chat for the next few days via text before he asked me if I wanted to meet in person.

He had gotten my attention with his messages, but I was still unsure of what he looked like when he asked me to meet up with him. So on the night of our first date, I was tired from a jam-packed weekend in Nashville so I just threw on a tank top and jeans instead of my usual first-date dress. I had months of research that helped me figure out that my blue and white striped sundress was the right packaging for my summer dates since every guy I met gave me a compliment on it. They said it was "fun and cute". That's exactly what I want people to see when I'm coming their way! So, yes, I had a first-date dress.

But on this particular night, I wasn't feeling exceptionally fun because of my exhausting weekend and long day at work … until I walked in the door of the arcade bar. I saw him sitting at the bar and I immediately looked at my watch trying to figure out if I had enough time to run home to change into the first-date dress. Why didn't I wear the first-date dress?! Nope! He spotted me, so all I could do was start in with the stories I had prepared for the date as I was driving back from Nashville, and then hope for the best. To this day he still tells people that I wore a turtleneck on our first date. A turtleneck! He thought my outfit was so boring that he truly believes it was a turtleneck. More proof that packaging really does help tell your story and that first impression is what will be remembered. Their first impression. Their perception of you. If you want that to match who you really are, then make sure what you look like on the outside reflects who you are on the inside.

Dating is marketing. I believe this with all of my heart. Because of this, I've jotted down some of the advice I live by so you can easily reference it when you are crafting your own marketing plan for finding the one. There are so many other marketing principles that can work in dating, so I would love to chat with you more about them. Because you purchased this book, you are invited to join my private Facebook Community where you will have direct access to me, as well as people across the country who are sharing their dating stories in hopes that we can all learn from them. It's a place where positive people come together to support each other. If you would like to join the group, please drop me an email at Tracie@HitzAndBranding.com. I can't wait to meet you!

Dating Is Marketing Advice

- Tell a True Story

- Identify Your Target Market

- Define Your Avatar

- Stop Mass Marketing

- Create Your Elevator Pitch

- Quiet Your Inner Mean Girl

- Done is Better Than Perfect
- Calculate Your ROI

- Work on Know, Like, And Trust
- Provide Value

- Be Interesting

- Cut Your Losses

- Incentivize the Customer

- Paint a Picture of the Future

- Assemble Your Board of Directors

- Have Flash Sales

- Write a Catchy Slogan
- Perfect Your Packaging

CHAPTER ELEVEN

DATING IS TAKING ACTION

Just like me, it's unlikely that your marketing plan will work every time. Building your brand is a process because you are always evolving, so learning these marketing techniques will help tell your story even as it changes. By checking in with yourself frequently, you will be more prepared to market your way to even more first dates. Maybe as you are reading this book you are already noticing that marketing has been part of your dating process too. Just like 16-year-old Tracie, who wrote a marketing plan to get a Vice Versa date without even knowing that's what she was doing. Back then, I just set my goal, created a plan, and told my story for whatever I was going after. It worked to land that first date that I still cherish to this day. I saw something I wanted, and I went after it with everything I had. Just like my parents taught me.

Even though so much has changed in the dating world in the last 25 years, the same process still applies. It doesn't matter if there are new ways to meet people always popping up as technology advances as long as you keep adjusting your plan. Be open to these new opportunities. You can use any one of those avenues out there to show someone that you are interesting. You should also lean on those around you who love and support you. It's not desperate to ask for help to meet someone. I've found that it's harder to find that perfect person than it is to find the perfect job, so why do we ask for job help, but not dating help? If you're like me, you don't have any trouble asking someone to look over your resume or make a call on your behalf to get a job, so don't hesitate to ask your friends to do the same with your dating profile or setting you up on a date.

Think about who you would put on your Personal Board of Directors. That diverse group of people in your life who are influencers. The people who aren't afraid to take action. In addition to your core group of people who know you better than anyone, reach out to that friend who is always posting photos with groups of girls or that friend who works at a male-dominated company. Include people who have access to single people.

You will also need that friend who will do absolutely anything. The friend that has no fear so you have someone to help you step outside your comfort zone to try new things and talk to everyone along the way. That friend who will quiet your inner voice. Assemble the best wingmen and women. Think about the qualities you need in these people so you always have someone who is encouraging you to take action and pushing you to go farther than you ever thought was possible.

I don't actually hold board meetings because that might be a little extreme, but I do check in regularly with my Personal Board of Directors individually. For me, the best form of communication to keep them updated on my life so I stay top of mind is social media. I think of my social media as my personal newsletter. My annual report. My dating resume. Facebook calls them status updates on your wall, and that's exactly how you should treat every post no matter what social media platforms you use. Keep people updated on who you are and where you are going so they know how to help you get there.

This means you need a social media strategy as part of your marketing plan. Before you post, ask yourself if this helps tell your story. Try not to share too often. A couple times a week on Facebook, everyday on Instagram, and several times a day is okay on SnapChat and Twitter. Don't share vague thoughts that sound like something's wrong or make you sound negative. Update your cover photo whenever you have the most amazing moment. Then, at the end of the year, you can go back to your cover photos for self-reflection. Be intentional about what you post. The next three pages are examples of my Facebook posts when I was trying to get the turtleneck guy's attention. Silly, sweet, and ambitious posts. Don't-you-want-to-be-in-my-life posts?

Tracie Hitz shared a photo.
October 11, 2016 ·

RIP Mike the Tiger. Such a cool tradition in college football.

Tracie Hitz is at Maryland Stadium.
November 12, 2016 ·

Just one of the many "courses" at the Maryland Football tailgate vs OSU. These turkey legs were a great warmup for Thanksgiving!

Tracie Hitz added a new photo — at IU Football Tailgating Fields.
November 26, 2016

Oh, I remember the days of working on football Saturdays. I've definitely adjusted to being on the other side, although I do miss the golf cart.

Tracie Hitz shared a photo.
December 19, 2016

Good times being the featured #GirlBoss today!

The Relish
December 18, 2016

Tracie Hitz updated her cover photo.
January 30, 2017 · 🌐 ▾

One of the many things I miss is just how nice my brother was. As the crowd gathered around to watch us play Pong years ago, he was genuinely happy for me after I beat him in an epic best-of-three battle. He didn't even care that I had such an obnoxious victory dance ... he just laughed that awesome laugh. Gone three years tomorrow, but thank goodness his lessons still live on ... and one of these days I might actually win and/or lose with grace. Maybe.

Tracie Hitz added a new photo — at Hacienda de la Cruz.
April 10, 2017 · Cabo San Lucas, Mexico · 👥

Last day in Cabo. I don't know how we can ever top this trip. Thanks again, Mark and Hector!

Social media is an amazing place to tell your story to your "tribe", as Godin calls those people who can spread your message. If you don't share your idea, your goals, or your mission, then your tribe can't help you make it happen. If you don't remind people that you're single and that you're awesome, they can't help to expand your reach to more single people. If you aren't on social media, please don't skip over this section. Instead, read it to then decide whether it's worth jumping on at least one social media platform to connect with your tribe.

If you are confident in who you are and living your best life with a purpose, then it should be easy to post interesting tidbits a few times a week. Whether it's a photo, a quote, or an article, share it with your people. If you have a date that didn't go the way you wanted, post about it to remind people that you are still looking. Be sure to stay positive with your story because no one wants to set their friends up with someone who trashes people after a date. People are reluctant to play matchmaker in the first place, so show that you are worth the time and effort they've taken to do so. You want to keep popping into their social media feeds so you are the first person they think of when someone asks them if they know any single people. By telling your story on social media, your friends are now ready to share your elevator pitch instead of being forced to say something generic.

"Um, yeah. I have a single friend. She's nice, has a job, and her hair is brown."

That's not interesting. When my friends were selling me, I wanted them to be specific.

"I have the most amazing friend. She's always popping around the country attending sporting events and concerts, she's crushing her job, she's thoughtful, and always makes me laugh."

The only way they will say this about me is if I share those parts of my life with them. Trying to convince someone to go on a blind date isn't always easy, so give people the info they need to close the deal for you. Look at your SWOT analysis, identify your brand, and tell your story to everyone you can every chance you get. This is not desperate. This is marketing. This is dating.

Using social media as a dating resume also means that you are ready for anyone to pop on there, not just your friends when they are looking for that perfect photo to share with a potential date. Most of the guys I matched with online jumped on social media to dig into my life. Even though my Facebook page was fairly locked down, they could still see profile pictures and cover photos even if I didn't accept their friend request. After I confirmed one guy's friend request, I went for a run and before I even finished, he sent a text message saying he thought it would be best to just be friends. And let me tell you, I don't run very fast and I definitely don't run very far, so in less than 30 minutes, he made up his mind about me. So what was on my Facebook wall that turned him off? It was actually what turned him on. All of my beautiful friends who were in the cover photos with me. Those cover photos that document my most amazing memories through the years. I know these photos are what caused his change in behavior because he actually texted that to me.

"UR friends are smoking hot. Let's all hang out this weekend."

It was clear he did his own ROI calculations and saw my value as someone who could introduce him to multiple dates instead gambling on one date with me. He saw me as an opportunity, or so he thought. He didn't factor in that when I told my friends what he said, they wanted nothing to do with him. This interaction could've swayed me into thinking that my friends are actually a threat when it comes to dating. Because they are younger, thinner, and prettier than me, I might lose guys to them if I keep them on my Facebook page. But that's just silly. These ladies actually helped me weed this guy out and they didn't even need to meet him. This saved me that time, energy, and frustration that comes along with dating. This is more proof that rejection isn't a bad thing!

There are so many ways to put yourself out there now, which means the chances of being rejected have definitely multiplied. When I compare my Vice Versa Dance Marketing Plan to what is now my Dating Is Marketing Plan it can seem overwhelming with all of the new avenues available to meet someone. More isn't always better, but it's definitely a benefit in this case because it allows you to diversify your plan, as well as find the mediums that you feel the most comfortable using. If online dating isn't for you, you can always find other ways to get your message out there. Creating a good marketing mix expands your reach and can keep you from getting frustrated if your main marketing avenue isn't working as quickly as you hoped. I've compiled a list of ways that you can meet someone, so take a look to see what resonates with your character.

ATTEND LOCAL EVENTS

Subscribe to email newsletters, search social media, and go online so you always know what events are happening in your town, like flea markets, taste of the town festivals, concerts, etc. This is a great way to find a person with similar passions, which gives you easy conversation starters when someone catches your eye. Set a goal for the number of events you want to attend each month so you make dating a priority.

DO WHAT YOU LOVE (A LOT)

This goes hand-in-hand with "Attend Events", but it's even more targeted because it includes smaller activities that are typically put on in a series so you get that repetition with the same people, which is often more comfortable when you're in a new setting. I found the most success in joining rec leagues. I played co-ed soccer, dodgeball, and sand volleyball in my late 20s several times a week. Because teams were usually short on girls, I would often sub on multiple teams a night, which expanded my reach beyond just my team. Then, in my 30s I switched to mini-golf, cornhole, and shuffleboard leagues. I also enjoyed taking classes like piano, photography, and cooking.

Most towns have trivia and bingo nights that are great for all ages. If your city has meet up groups, jump online to see if there is a group doing something that you enjoy, like book clubs, wine nights, or movie groups. If you don't meet anyone along the way, that's okay because you're still doing things that you love so there is no wasted time when you're investing in yourself. You may even meet another wingman or woman to join your Personal Board of Directors along the way.

ENJOY EVERYDAY LIFE

You can meet people during your daily routine at the grocery store, at church, or even when you're using public transportation. One of my favorite places to meet people was at airports, either before the flight or on the plane. It's a great opportunity to sell yourself when you are sitting next to someone during a long flight. Southwest has been great for this because you can pick your own seat. You can strike up a conversation at the gate to sit together or you can find them once they are on the plane.

The key with meeting someone while you are enjoying everyday life is to engage. A simple smile can change everything. Making eye contact with someone across the room at the coffee shop or even going to a restaurant early to sit at the bar while you wait for your friends makes you approachable to anyone who may be trying to get up the courage to talk to you. Giving any sign that you are up for chatting will put people at ease so they are more likely to take that risk by starting a conversation. With your encouragement, they will assume that they will be met with kindness.

Part of being approachable is your packaging. Even if it's an early morning flight, resist the urge to roll into the airport in your pajamas.

JOIN ADVENTURE OR SOCIAL CLUBS

I worked part time at a social club in my 20s, so I know these can be amazing places to connect with people if you engage at the events. The company plans everything, provides a mix of people to meet, and makes sure that everyone there is single. That last part is huge. Being surrounded by single people is amazing, but it can also be intimidating for members because they felt pressure every time they talked to someone. They thought every conversation they had at an event was make or break in getting a date, so it didn't always feel casual. Because of this, I spent a lot of time talking to the members in an effort to help them feel more comfortable in this environment. Those who did the prep work in advance had more success meeting people at the events because they felt at ease talking about themselves. They also made friends with people in the club, which made the events more fun to attend while expanding their social circle so they could go out without using the club every time. If run well, the cost of these clubs can be worth the expense because they provide consistent opportunities to get in front of people that you might not be able to meet on your own. Like everything else, it's up to you to make something happen if you join a social club.

USE DATING SERVICES

In a time where everything seems to be going online, there are still dating services around the country that facilitate meeting in person. You will have someone dedicated to helping you throughout the process so you can stay motivated to find the one. While there is also a cost associated with these services, calculate that ROI to see if it's worth your time to have someone else handle everything for you or if you can create a plan to do it on your own. If you decide to use a service, be sure to have your story together to share with these professionals so they can set you up with your best matches. They will become one of the most important people in your tribe.

ATTEND LIVE DATING EVENTS
There are companies that host one-off events, like speed dating where you don't have to commit to a monthly or yearly membership. This allows you to test things out to see what works. A great place to look for these types of events is on Eventbrite. I enjoyed my experiences with speed dating because they put you in the room with single people, usually segmented by age, which is helpful to get more targeted. This gives you opportunities to meet several people at one time to practice telling your story.

In addition to these quick events, there are also singles cruises and day trips that give you a little more time with people in a laid back setting. Experiment with the different events, including ones that might take you out of your comfort zone. Take note of where your ideal avatar appears to be hanging out so you can continue to sign up for those types of events. Choose to be positive even if you run into unkind people along the way. Not everyone is prepared for these events, so use your knowledge to help them shift their attitude so that dating is fun!

ENGAGE IN ONLINE DATING

The stigma that comes with online dating can keep people away from taking a chance on it, but the premise is the same as live dating events and social clubs in that these platforms are getting you in front of single people. It doesn't matter how you meet someone. Use every avenue that you can to find your avatar. You may hear negative stories about people who have met online, but it doesn't matter if you meet someone in person or online, you are bound to come across a few mean people. They are everywhere. But don't discount the whole online world because of a few bad apples. You absolutely will go on "bad" dates with people, but most of the time you can avoid this by weeding these people out on the front end using your best questions. When your conversations center around your core values you can usually determine whether someone is worth your time, money, and energy. This will keep the misses to a minimum, but if it is flop you are still practicing, learning, and growing for the next one.

Please don't let what others think about online dating keep you from using it. Don't be embarrassed to tell people that you met someone online. It's just a platform that connects people in a world that is reliant on the virtual space. There is so much more to gain than there is to lose by opening yourself up to online dating. If you add this platform to your marketing plan, you can track the progress and evaluate if it's worth your time. If not, cross it off the list and concentrate on the platforms that work best for you. For YOU. This is your journey.

ATTEND NETWORKING EVENTS

Members of your Personal Board of Directors should be working to set you up on dates or going out with you to find someone. Professional networking events are a great way to do just that. There are local events every month in most cities, but sometimes it's worth the trip to go to events outside of your city, especially work conferences that connect people in your industry. Two of my boyfriends were the results of turning a work connection at a conference into a long distance relationship. The marketing plans went from email to texting to FaceTime to in-person weekends together. We connected quickly because we had an understanding of the lifestyle that goes along with working in the sports industry. We were ambitious people trying to figure out how a relationship would fit inside our jam-packed lives. This was an extremely effective way to share our stories because we knew what it was like to live that life, especially being able to lean on each other for that career advice and support.

BE ACTIVE ON SOCIAL MEDIA

You never know who will stumble upon your photo on social media. When a friend posts a photo with you, hundreds of people are likely to see it. Sometimes thousands depending on how many friends they have, as well as the friends of the other people tagged in the photo. Like that guy who decided not to date me because my friends were hotter, showing up on social media garners attention from people you might not meet otherwise. Every time I post a photo of my beautiful friends, my guy friends will message me asking if they are single. Every. Time. The same could happen to you if you are getting out there, taking photos, and showing the world that you are living your best life. Posting a photo is easy.

There are several ways to use social media to get attention, so test out what works for you. Facebook and Instagram both show my entire life while Twitter and LinkedIn are strictly professional. SnapChat is just for the funniest parts of my life. You can experiment with what works, but let's all make sure to keep LinkedIn a professional platform as it was originally intended. It was not meant to be used to reach out to random people in hopes of getting a date, so those who use it this way are often met with resistance.

Twitter on the other hand can be used for sharing news articles, professional development, and personal updates, so depending on how people use it, Twitter can be a great way to build relationships. I dated two guys that I met on Twitter. We started noticing each other when we popped into the same Twitter chats with several mutual friends in the industry. After a few weeks of commenting on their updates, they tested the waters by sending me direct messages. Then, text messages turned into FaceTime before we started hanging out in person. They both lived hundreds of miles away, but at that time in my life I was looking for a change of cities, so it was worth it for me to see if anything would come of these new connections. Consistently checking in on where you are in life and where you want to go will guide you to make decisions that fit that time in your life. If I hadn't checked in with myself, I might have missed out on dating those two wonderful people.

People thought I was crazy to meet up with these strangers because they didn't see how it would ever work. Plus, some were worried the guys might have bad intentions because we connected on Twitter, but I vetted both of them through friends first so I knew I would be okay. These guys knew people in my tribe, so Twitter was just another platform to meet them. My Personal Board of Directors always help me think through all angles of a situation or opportunity, so while some shared their concerns about meeting this way, they ultimately supported my decision to take this leap. One of them made me text her every hour on the hour to make sure I was still alive. And that wasn't even my mom. I'm telling you, that lady knows how to support me like no other! Surround yourself with people who aren't going to hold you back, but instead will push you to see what's possible. Taking a risk is scary, but if it's calculated and you have people around you, that makes it a little easier to put yourself out there.

Through my decades of dating, I've tried a lot of different ways to meet people for friendships, business relationships, and boyfriends. Being open to the changes that happened through the years allowed me to find avenues that worked for me. I never thought I would meet someone on Twitter or would love dating apps, but these are just platforms to start conversations, and that's what I love. As long as you are taking action consistently, you will also find success. Once you have your goal set, write down the tactics that will help you get there. Keep an open mind. Tune everybody out. Believe that it will happen.

Dating Is Taking Action

- [ ] Attend Local Events
- [ ] Do What You Love (A Lot)
- [ ] Enjoy Everyday Life
- [ ] Join Adventure Club of Social Club
- [ ] Use Dating Services
- [ ] Attend Live Dating Events
- [ ] Engage in Online Dating
- [ ] Attend Networking Events
- [ ] Be Active on Social Media
- [ ]
- [ ]
- [ ]
- [ ]
- [ ]

CHAPTER TWELVE

DATING IS ROUTINE

Now that you have a list of proven ways to meet someone, think about any other avenues that are available to you in your town and beyond. Add them to the list on the previous page. Look over this list of dating resources so you can decide which ones resonate with you. Determine what feels natural, promising, and fun. What do you believe you can follow through on each month? Put a checkmark next to everything that you would be willing to do consistently. Figure out what you can fit into your routine. If you don't have as much time as you think you need, what can you cut out of your routine to make room? Decide how much of a priority it is to meet someone. What time are you willing to put into it?

Now, take another look at the list and pick one idea that completely pushes you outside your comfort zone. That one thing that makes you cringe a little thinking about it. That's the one! Put a checkmark next to it so you can commit to trying something you've never done. Commit to this avenue for at least one month. By committing, I mean actively doing something everyday or every week with that medium so it becomes comfortable. Quiet your inner voice by researching, reflecting, and preparing. Everything is less scary when you're ready to attack it. Add all of these ideas into your (Andre Agassi) calendar so you are consistently working on meeting new people instead of binging your time here and there trying to find someone. Consistency and frequency are huge contributing factors to the success of a dating marketing plan.

Planning in advance and creating a routine allows you to calculate how much time you have and/or want to spend each week actively marketing yourself for a date. Being smart with your time will limit your frustration while also making dating a priority in your life. Sure, sometimes we fall into a great job or the perfect date, but when you really want something in life, you'll definitely get results if you put forth the effort. This means blocking time on your calendar so you can work smart and stay committed to your goal. It's similar to a weight loss plan where you set your workout schedule each week, prepare your meals, and keep a food journal to make sure you are sticking to the plan. You make adjustment as you go. If you need a rest day or a cheat day to stay motivated, that's okay. Just don't let it throw you off of your overall routine.

I would often create dating challenges, write down how they went, and then sum up the lesson learned from the experience. As I got older, finding single guys got harder. In my early 30s, I would go on two dates in one day. When I turned 40, I worked hard just to get one date a month. But while I thought 12 dates wasn't a lot, my friends were complaining about how they hadn't gone on any dates that year. I was working to get those dates while they were waiting for them to happen. Challenge yourself!

Hitz & Mrs Journal

October 11:
I decided to challenge myself by seeing how quickly I could match with someone online and then meet up with him in person ... 35 minutes.

Met up with him to watch the Cubs' playoff game. After he left, he started sending inappropriate messages. I unmatched him by 12:30 am.

Lesson learned - the vibe that went along with wanting to meet up so quickly appeared to mean that I was interested in hooking up, not a relationship.

Having a trainer to support you and hold you accountable can produce better results in weight loss, and the same is true for dating. You can find that support system within your Personal Board of Directors, through some of the dating resources that will assign someone to you, or hiring a dating trainer to help you stay on track. If you need help, be sure to email me at Tracie@HitzAndBranding.com to join my private Facebook Community at no additional cost as a thank you for purchasing this book. This group was created to bring the readers together so we can share experiences that will keep people motivated and spread kindness along the way. You will learn tips like allotting 15 minutes when you first wake up every morning to check the dating apps for matches or scroll through Eventbrite to see what's going on in your town that week. Both of those practices were part of my morning routine. Then, my night routine was focused on returning my messages to people I matched with online. I usually did this while I ate dinner because that allowed me to be more efficient as I focused on just returning messages at that time. My dating routine was similar to an assembly line because I was able to separate my tasks out instead of trying to do a bunch all at once. It's difficult to multitask, so being focused on one thing at a time allowed me to be much more effective. It's like that assembly line that was first used by Henry Ford when he was making Ford's Model T. Just another life lesson I took away from Ford cars.

Trying to multitask would usually leave me feeling like I hadn't accomplished anything. While I liked my system, I found that guys were getting frustrated by me because I wasn't checking the app as often as they were so my response time wasn't fast enough for most. If they sent a message after 9 pm, it was unlikely that I would see it until the next night. We had different routines, but without knowing that, sometimes they would go on the offensive before I even had the chance to respond. One night, I sat down for dinner to check my messages and a guy started and ended a conversation without me even knowing it.

9:02 pm – Hey

11:17 pm – Hello?!

9:33 am – Screw you!

I tried not to take this personally because it was obvious we had different routines and expectations. Per usual, it also seemed like these guys were projecting some past experiences on me, but this type of response still didn't feel great when I would sit down for dinner to read messages like this. Yes, this "conversation" happened multiple times. These guys weeded themselves out without any interaction from me at all. For those who yelled at me, but then didn't unmatch me, I did reply letting them know that I hadn't checked my messages, so in the future they may want to have a little more patience. I also let them know that their words were hurtful, and that I hoped they would think twice before doing that to someone else. They never responded back.

I created a routine to make sure the dating process was fun for me and for those I encountered. While it sounds like being so structured would be the opposite of fun, being efficient with my time made me happy. Meeting new people, enjoying your home city, or traveling to new ones should absolutely be fun. You have the ability to make dating whatever you want it to be. At the core of most dating frustration is communication. Like in the messages above, that guy expected me to write back immediately because that's what he would've done, but that wasn't my routine.

Dating is Routine

Goal: Go on at least one date per month before turning 41 years old

Sunday:
- Watch NFL game in person or at bar
- Spend 15 minutes on dating app(s)
- Post photos on social media

Monday:
- Spend 30 minutes on dating app(s)
- Scroll things to do around town

Tuesday:
- Go to Shuffleboard League OR
- Reserved for potential first date
- Spend 5 minutes on dating app(s)

Wednesday:
- Dinner with friends
- Spend 15 minutes on dating app(s)

Thursday:
- Girls' Night Out
- Spend 5 minutes on dating app(s)
- Post to social media

Friday:
- Spend 60 minutes on dating app(s)

Saturday:
- Attend event or go out with friends
- Post to social media

Part of a routine includes their communication style. Some people are more engaging when they talk on the phone than they are via text, so they might push for jumping on a call while the other person thinks that's uncomfortable. If people aren't using their preferred form of communication, it can keep them from sharing their story effectively. I personally hate talking on the phone, but I usually agree to it when they ask in hopes that they will feel comfortable so there's a better chance that we will get to know each other faster.

Effective communication also includes sharing expectations about a potential relationship. Some people are more serious than others when it comes to settling down, so knowing those different goals in advance is extremely helpful to navigate at the beginning. With the reputation dating apps have for being an avenue for people to just hook up, some people stay away from trying them at all, including me for a while. I finally decided to give them a try when I turned 40, but I definitely proceeded with caution. I added dating apps into my marketing plan, which significantly increased the number of people I met that year. Of course, there absolutely were guys on the apps that just wanted to hook up, but most of them weren't trying to hide it so I was able to make good decisions. The people in open relationships usually shared that information up front with some using their wedding photos as their profile pictures.

It can be difficult to build a relationship if your goals aren't aligned, so even if you find your groove with the communication avenues, you can still be off when it comes to where you are headed. When I finally made the commitment to use the dating apps, I decided to go all in for the next year to meet as many guys as possible in hopes of finding my person. I was finally ready to settle down, so I was clear about my intentions when I was trying to figure out who to invest my time, money, and energy into that year. I wrote down my goal and tactics so I could see them everyday and then make adjustments as I went along.

I was focused on making something happen in those 365 days.

This is 40 Plan

Goal: Go on at least one date a month from August - July

Tactic: Join Tinder and engage everyday

Tactic: Join Bumble if necessary

Tactic: Join at least one rec league

Tactic: Attend networking events

Tactic: Eat out alone once a week

Tactic: Plan girls' night once a week

My goal was to have at least one date a month with one of those guys being someone I could date long term by the end of that year. I adjusted my dating plan to be more intentional because I wanted to find my perfect match. And I did, just in time. Two weeks before my 41st birthday, I decided to go on that final date of the year even though I was exhausted and wasn't sure what the guy looked like. That guy who I didn't think warranted my fun and cute first-date dress. You know, the guy who swears I was wearing a turtleneck on our first date. I even made sure the meeting place was fun just in case he wasn't, so we met at an arcade bar. This was my last date before the year was up, so cancelling wasn't really an option even though I thought about it. If I hadn't written my goal down, I probably would've bailed on this date, but I'm so glad that I stayed committed to my plan. From the moment I sat down, we laughed until our faces hurt. That went on for several months even though he was very clear from the beginning that he wasn't ready for a relationship. If he had written down a goal, I imagine it would've looked something like this.

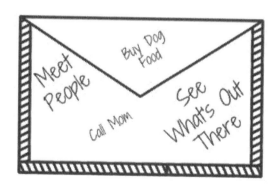

He had only been on the dating app for a couple of weeks when we matched. I found out early on that he only got on there to take his mind off of his recent breakup. His friends told him to get on the app because "people don't actually date anyone on there." They told him to just have fun. And we did! But I was treating everything like a relationship while he just thought of me as a fun distraction. After three months, I decided to have that difficult conversation even though I knew that I didn't want to actually hear what he had to say. I knew that confronting him about being on two different pages would likely end in heartbreak, but I couldn't keep pretending that everything was okay on my end. I was way too invested in him because I had finally found someone who I connected with deeply, so I had to have this conversation. I needed to cut my losses if he told me there was no future. I knew he felt something special with me too, but he definitely wasn't ready to admit it to me or even to himself. He was still holding on to his past. After that conversation, he decided that it was best that we didn't see each other anymore because we wanted different things. He was trying to keep from hurting me, but that conversation hurt. A lot. But he was right that it was what we needed to do. We weren't going to end up in the same place at this time at this rate.

But because of the insight he shared in that conversation, I didn't give up completely. He acknowledged there was something between us, so while he would no longer hang out with me, I stayed positive that he would come around because it seemed like what was keeping us apart was just timing. I took a break, but that was just so I could adjust my marketing plan. We didn't see each other for six months, but we texted almost everyday. Despite 99% of my friends telling me to rip the Band-Aid off completely to just let him go, I was determined to tell my story to him until he was ready to truly listen. Or until he shut the door on the possibility.

I was living my best life while we were on this break, and I was sure to post the highlights on Facebook and SnapChat so he could see them. I used SnapChat specifically because you can track on who looks at your posts, and he always did. Always. I was in his daily routine. At the end of those six months, he came by my house unexpectedly one night. I couldn't believe it. He was getting closure on his last relationship. He stopped listening to his friends. He was figuring out what he wanted. We were getting on the same page.

We worked through the conflict in our story that led to the most amazing resolution. It was the ending I believed in all along. I believed it because we had that difficult conversation six months earlier. If he hadn't been honest with me that day, I would've thought he was a jerk just like the rest of my friends. I would've deleted his number and kicked him off my social media. Instead, I collected all of the information surrounding our relationship because I wanted to make the best decision. I wanted to make a decision based on facts rather than guesses. Communication takes that guesswork out of the situation. It's hard to be vulnerable, especially early on in a relationship, but sharing your true feelings is a game changer even if that means you will encounter a little heartbreak along the way. Figure out which risks to take by having open communication, and be patient when you find someone worth waiting for.

CHAPTER THIRTEEN

DATING IS KINDNESS

What a different dating world it would be if everyone communicated openly so we wouldn't waste our time, money, or energy on relationships that are going nowhere. If people stopped ghosting, "the practice of ending a personal relationship with someone by suddenly and without explanation withdrawing from communication" and/or breadcrumbing, "the act of leading someone on by contacting them intermittently – be that by phone or social media – to keep them interested", our self confidence would grow instead of take a hit each time.

Kindness goes a long way. Have you ever given a compliment to a stranger? It's such an amazing feeling. When I lived in Chicago, I told a woman on the street that she looked beautiful, and she almost started crying when she thanked me.

"You don't know how much I needed to hear that today."

This woman, who looked like she had the most amazing life, was affected when I said what I was thinking instead of keeping it inside. Giving that compliment was easy because I meant it, but also because there wasn't anything at stake for me in saying it. If I was going to give a compliment to a guy I was interested in, it would take a ten-minute pep talk to myself, and I still might not get the courage up to actually say it. Being brave enough to say something is how we start that process of know, like, and trust that can help us build a relationship. Making that first move is risky because we don't know how people will react. From past experiences, I know there's a really good chance that they will react negatively. It's that negativity that can hold us back from making connections with those who actually would be grateful for the interaction.

Creating a routine that forces you to learn how to talk to strangers everyday will build that confidence in yourself so you will want to take these risks. The more you practice, the less risky these encounters will feel. These risks will eventually become your new normal. If you think my confidence soared after getting my first boyfriend in high school, you are wrong. I was still the shyest person in America, maybe even the world, for quite a bit of my life. So shy that when I got my first full-time job, I stayed at the office until 9 pm just to record my voicemail greeting because I didn't want other people to hear me in case I made a mistake. That shyness used to be my norm, but after years of practice, now I will talk to anyone, anytime, about anything. People were still mean from time-to-time, but I just return it with kindness. It can completely turn the conversation around. Even when I wasn't trying to get a date, people weren't always nice. I believe that if someone is nasty for no apparent reason, they must have had something happen to them in their past that is still affecting them today. If my response is always kindness, I hope I can help them move forward. Start fresh. I hope this book helps you move forward towards whatever it is that you want in life. I would be so grateful if you helped others do the same, especially in the dating world.

Even going on a "bad" date can be an opportunity to make a difference. We can choose to take the time to turn it into a positive. Like a first date I went on when I was visiting Nashville. As I parked my car, I sent a quick text letting him know that I was walking up to the restaurant. His response had me rethinking everything I thought I knew about him.

"Cool. I already ordered."

I stopped walking. I started laughing. Then, I sent a group text to members of my Personal Board of Directors, who all responded within seconds. That quick response rate is definitely one of the many reasons they are all on my Board of Directors!

"Sounds like an a-hole. Go home right now."

"Turn around and RUN."

"Please tell me you're not going in. Of course, you're going in."

I thought about their comments, and that last friend was right ... of course I went in. I made this decision based on sheer curiosity. What type of guy would order his meal before his date got to the restaurant? I wasn't even late! I just had to find out. I thought about the ROI, which was simple. I was really hungry and I was excited to spend an afternoon outside listening to music in one of my favorite cities. Even if this guy turned out to be as ridiculous as it now appeared, I felt like I would still have fun doing something I enjoy. Plus, it's another opportunity to practice telling my story. He didn't know it, but that one text he sent actually communicated his expectations for the date, and I felt no pressure as I went into the restaurant. He obviously wasn't taking this date as seriously as I had intended. Our goals didn't appear to be lining up. When I walked up to the table, he had a bucket of beer in front of him, and he kind of looked like he'd been hit by a truck.

"Rough night?"

Had he not sent that text, there's no way I would've started our conversation like that, but he had tossed himself into the friend zone so I changed my game plan. He said he was so hung over that he hoped drinking some beer and eating greasy food would help him recover in time for this date. Plot twist! In his mind, he was doing a good thing by ordering his food and drinks before I got there. He didn't even consider how that gesture could be perceived by the other person. When I heard this explanation I thought he could've ordered an appetizer to help with his hangover because that could look like he was being thoughtful by having something for us to share when I arrived. His text could've said, "Cool. I already ordered an appetizer. Can I get you a drink?" That would've changed everything in my mind. Everyone brings a different point of view into a situation.

Based on the text responses, my Personal Board of Directors seemed to have similar points of view, so I had to update them after the date. When I told them that I felt an appetizer would've changed things, one friend said that she still would've been annoyed if he ordered food for her on a first date because she doesn't need a man telling her what to eat. Having an appetizer waiting for me at the table seemed like heaven to me, but she saw it as him taking away her independence. You just never know what the other person will bring with them to the date. So before you turn around to run from a strange situation, take a breath, and then take a chance on kindness. That is exactly what I learned from that date. There are no bad dates if you take something away that will help you become better, and hopefully you can help others along the way.

So I sat down at the table where I awkwardly watched him eat his burger and fries. Then, he awkwardly watched me eat my food. Once the food was gone, we actually ended up having a pretty good time. It was a gorgeous day, the music was amazing, and the drinks were flowing. I could've had fun with just about anyone in that setting because I set up the date that way. I created a date that I wanted to go on, and it didn't really matter with who. I decided to go out on another date and that's where it became apparent that he truly was an inconsiderate person. Like when he loudly shared his political opinions that were not only offending me, but were so clearly offending those around us. I decided to go on a third date with him because that month I had created another challenge for myself where I was going to give each guy at least three dates before I made a decision. I've been called picky all my life. I call it efficient. Regardless, I saw it as a learning experience to see if more dates led to different results. It didn't.

One member of my Personal Board of Directors met up with us for our third date that I turned into a group date for a football game I really wanted to attend. On the date I chatted with her about my concerns to make sure I wasn't being overly sensitive. But when we came back from the ladies room, he made it clear that he wasn't a nice person. He was trying to talk the hostess into bumping us up on the wait list for a table at the extremely busy restaurant, but she wasn't budging.

"Well, that's what I expected from a fatass like you."

I was mortified when I heard this walking up to him. I just kept walking. I was so angry that I couldn't even put any words together. My friend stopped at the hostess stand thinking I would come back, but I inadvertently left her behind as I was trying to make sense of the comment. My friend walked out a few minutes later. We decided that I wouldn't be able to say anything constructive to him in person because I was too upset, so we crafted a text message that we hoped would resonate on some level with him. I wanted to let him know that wasn't okay to treat someone like that. No matter what happened in his past, that woman did not deserve those words. Not surprisingly, he fired back some rude comments to me and I tried again to explain how hurtful his words were. It didn't work that night, but I still hold out hope that at some point he thought about those terrible words and decided to make a change in how he treats people. If we can all stay positive in even the worst situations maybe we can make a bigger change.

There were several other dates similar to this, and the reason I still came out of them with a positive attitude is that I hope I can make an impact. I tell you these stories because I'm hopeful that together we can create a shift in the dating world. Some guys on these dates didn't seem to know that their actions were actually hurtful, not funny. One of the police officers I went on a date with was complaining about work, which is one of my favorite things to analyze. He said that his boss didn't like him. I was fascinated by this comment because that kind of statement can be so telling about a person. It was first date gold for me! When I asked why, he told me that his boss doesn't think his jokes are funny. Now, I think just about everything is funny, so I asked for examples of the jokes he told at work. He then clarified that they were more like pranks.

"I see the same prostitutes every day during my shift, so we usually put them in the car and drop them off into the next county so we don't have to deal with them. It's a game we play with the other cops. We move these women back and forth almost everyday. As we are driving up to them, we like to make up songs that we sing over the speaker. One of my favorites is, 'Guess who's a prostitute? A dirty, nasty prostitute?' They always get so mad."

Before I can put words together to respond, he goes on to tell me about another "prank" he does when he pulls people over for speeding.

"For high school kids, we make them get out of the car so we can search it. Then, we put one of our guns in the backseat, pull it out, and pretend that we found it in the car. They almost crap their pants. It is so hilarious."

I spent the rest of the date mentoring him about why his boss, and most people, wouldn't think this is funny. I found his actions inappropriate in general, but to have someone who is supposed to serve and protect us being so disrespectful was maddening. The expectation that goes along with wearing that uniform was not one that he was upholding. When I shared my thoughts with him, I could see that I was getting through to him a little, so I encouraged him to meet with his boss for guidance so he can grow in the job, the uniform, and hopefully life. I wished him the best and crossed my fingers that I never got pulled over during his shift.

Through the years I've spent many dates giving advice about anything from buying a car to investing in a 401K. I love to help people. It's who I am at the core. I've even helped a few guys get dates with other women. Like that guy who swears I wore a turtleneck on our first date; even though I wanted to date him more than anything, during our break, I gave him advice on how to increase his matches on the dating apps. It was actually an accident at first when I let it slip out that his photo choices were decreasing his chances of meeting someone. When he asked what he should do, I decided to help him. He deleted the group photos and the one with his dog and replaced them with pictures of just him doing things he loved. He will be the first one to tell you that changing his photos helped him match with a lot more women. This wasn't easy for me to hear at the time, but chatting with these women is ultimately what contributed to him realizing that the connection we had was special. It was a little crazy to give him dating advice in my new role of "friend", but playing it safe is rarely the best option. When we first met, he told me his goal for getting on the dating apps was to "see what was out there", so that's what he needed to do before he would be ready for a relationship. It was a risk helping him meet more women, but I spent the first half of my life blending in, so now I spend my time trying to stand out from the crowd. Who's ready to join me?!

CHAPTER FOURTEEN

DATING IS BEING YOU

Your story is unique and needs to be shared with the world. Set yourself up for success by taking risks that are calculated and strategic. Take the time to check in with yourself to know who you are and what you want so you can create a great plan to get there. Learn from your past experiences, but don't let them hold you back when you see something you want. Don't let other people make you doubt yourself. Shake off the negativity and rejection so you can respond with kindness to stay positive on your journey. Take others with you who will support you and spread your message.

All of the experiences and all of the people who came in and out of my life in my first 25 years of dating had a hand in getting me where I am today. To who I am today. I've changed and grown along the way, so I made sure my goals were always in line with those changes. Always know what you want so you can stay focused on achieving it. For my high school boyfriend, he never wavered on his dream to be a father. To play baseball with his kids. That's ultimately what set us down different paths, but that's the way it was supposed to be. He's been married for over ten years now, has two kids, and coaches his son's baseball team. He set a goal and went after it with all of his heart, and I'm so proud of him for making it happen. Of course, his childhood dream of being a professional baseball player would've been pretty awesome too, but we grow, change, and adjust while staying true to our core values.

For me, I'm not writing for *Sports Illustrated*, but this book was also my dream. The joy I get from helping people write their own stories everyday is what I was meant to do. Being able to remind people how incredible they are is a gift. I love showing them that everything in life can be fun, especially dating. The ups and downs that come along with it are what build our character. That collection of qualities that tell our story is how we find that perfect person who connects with everything we are and plan to be.

Please use this book, my workshop guides, workshops, and more so you can make the time to look inside yourself to consistently check in on what drives you. Reflect on the dates that didn't go as planned to see what lessons you can take away to continue moving forward, and bring as many people along with you. Together, maybe we can shift the world forward with kindness, ambition, and a plan.

Limit the frustration you feel in dating by choosing to be happy. Commit to your plan, to being kind, and to taking action so nothing will hold you back from finding the one. Figure out who you want to be so you can find the person you want beside you as you continue to grow. It's a lot to take in. I'm sure it seems overwhelming. Maybe you think there isn't enough time to make things happen, but I assure you there is. Be intentional and strategic with your plan. Assemble your Personal Board of Directors. Create a routine. Continue to chip away.

You will absolutely make mistakes. You will run into people who make you doubt yourself. You will want to give up. But you won't. I know that you won't. You will look at your plan. You will look at yourself. You will take it one day at a time. You will find the one. I know this because once I started believing, ignoring, and planning, I saw a shift. When I walked into that arcade bar wearing a tank top (not a turtleneck!), I knew this was the person for me, even when he didn't know it yet. When my friends didn't believe it. I believed it. It wasn't an easy road back to each other, but my marketing plan was 100% the reason why we made it back. If you want to hear more about our story, our plan, and where we are now, please join my private Facebook Community. As a thank you for purchasing this book, you will receive access to this group along with all of the advice, support, and fun that comes along with it at no additional cost. Please send an email to Tracie@HitzAndBranding.com to request access. I'm so excited to meet every single one of you to hear your story so we can continue to write it together!

TRACIE HITZ

ABOUT THE AUTHOR

Tracie Hitz is a branding strategist with over 20 years of experience in the sports industry. She has worked with hundreds of college and professional sports teams to increase revenue and attendance through creative ideas that garner national attention.
She started her Hitz& Mrs. Blog in the ChicagoNow community through the Tribune Publishing Company in 2013. She's been using this platform to provide dating advice by showing the parallels between dating and marketing.
She is the Founder and CEO of Hitz & Branding, LLC where she works with personal and professional clients that span across all industries.
You can contact Hitz directly at Tracie@HitzAndBranding.com, subscribe to her blog at ChicagoNow.com/hitz-mrs, or follow her on social media at @HitzAndMrs (Twitter and Facebook) and @HitzAndMrsBlog (Instagram).

Made in the USA
Lexington, KY
31 January 2019